CELEBRATE
with CHOCOLATE

Other Books by Marcel Desaulniers

AN ALPHABET OF SWEETS

THE BURGER MEISTERS

DEATH BY CHOCOLATE

DEATH BY CHOCOLATE CAKES

DEATH BY CHOCOLATE COOKIES

DESSERTS TO DIE FOR

SALAD DAYS

THE TRELLIS COOKBOOK

CELEBRATE

with CHOCOLATE

TOTALLY OVER-THE-TOP RECIPES

MARCEL DESAULNIERS

Recipes with Ganache Hill Test Kitchen Chef Brett Bailey
and Trellis Pastry Chef Kelly Bailey –

Photographs by Ron Manville

WM

WILLIAM MORROW

An Imprint of HarperCollinsPublishers

CELEBRATE WITH CHOCOLATE. Copyright © 2002 by Marcel Desaulniers. All rights reserved. Printed in the United States of America. No part of this book may be used or reproduced in any manner whatsoever without written permission except in the case of brief quotations embodied in critical articles and reviews. For information address HarperCollins Publishers Inc., 10 East 53rd Street, New York, NY 10022.

HarperCollins books may be purchased for educational, business, or sales promotional use. For information please write: Special Markets Department, HarperCollins Publishers Inc., 10 East 53rd Street, New York, NY 10022.

FIRST EDITION

Designed by William Ruoto

Printed on acid-free paper

Library of Congress Cataloging-in-Publication Data has been applied for.

ISBN 0-688-16298-3

02 03 04 05 06 WBC/RRD 10 9 8 7 6 5 4 3 2 1

To my wife, Connie Desaulniers
Connie and chocolate make every day a celebration

CONTENTS

ACKNOWLEDGMENTS

Brett Bailey, Ganache Hill test kitchen chef
Kelly Bailey, Trellis pastry chef

Dan Green, literary agent
Harriet Bell, editor
Carrie Weinberg, publicist
Ron Manville, photographer

John and Julia Curtis, business partners
Penny Seu, editorial adviser

Michael Holdsworth, Trellis chef
Steve Francisco, Trellis senior assistant chef
Robert Cappetta, Trellis assistant chef
Jason Wade, Trellis assistant chef
Nicole Johnson, Trellis assistant pastry chef
The Trellis kitchen staff, management,
front-of-the-house, and office staff

Ed Wilhelm, photo intern
Donna Spilner, prop consultant

The students, instructors, and staff
at The Culinary Institute of America

CELEBRATE
with CHOCOLATE

INTRODUCTION

My love affair with chocolate makes me want to celebrate every day. More than a momentary sensation of pleasure, chocolate has enriched and distinguished my life. When I was a child, my mother's chocolate treats illuminated every conceivable holiday, including birthdays and Christmas, as well as everyday occasions such as staying home from school on a snowy day, or celebrating a cousin's return from the navy during the Korean conflict. As the years progressed, and this culinarily curious teenager turned his after-school work into an avocation, chocolate started speaking in different ways. More than a treat, chocolate became a passion.

However, my subsequent studies at The Culinary Institute of America, then located in New Haven, Connecticut, did not include much chocolate. The curriculum instead required us to learn the basics of culinary classics such as hollandaise and bouillabaisse. Baking and pastry making at that time were a modest part of the two-year program and mostly consisted of learning techniques from the primarily European instructors of making such staples as croissants, puff pastry, and pastillage (a modeling paste used to make elaborate decorations).

Although ganache made its entry later in my nascent career, by the time I reached the Culinary, I had learned enough about the mystique of chocolate from my mother that it became my entree to wooing the damsels of New Haven. Pity the neighboring "Yalies," for chocolate set me apart. Instead of studying together, my dates and I made chocolate treats, and we made sweet time.

After I'd graduated from the Culinary, Manhattan beckoned. Working with the best cooking talent in the country opened my eyes to ganache and its offspring, truffles. I knew I had found my calling. Alas, after only a few months into this part of life's journey, another call came—the draft. I had always dreamed of Paris, but not Parris Island, South Carolina. The flavors and aromas from the kitchens of New York were a far cry from those of the mess hall, where three times a day, indistinguishable monochromatic mush was plopped from a metal spoon onto metal plates held by grunts all in a row. And even more wretched, no chocolate (much less anything else pleasurable) could be found in boot camp.

Then came an all-expenses-paid trip to a former French colony in Southeast Asia, where chocolate again achieved supremacy, thanks to care packages from my mom filled with her chocolate chip cookies. Sharing those cookies made every package a celebration and gave me more prestige than my three stripes.

After my military meanderings, I found myself in Williamsburg, Virginia. Marriage, children, new jobs, birthdays and anniversaries, events such as the Kentucky Derby, and all manner of holidays (both secular and spiritual), gave me myriad opportunities for chocolate making and giving.

Now my life seems to be defined by chocolate. Books such as *Death by Chocolate* have brought success, infamy, and more reasons to create, consume, and enjoy chocolate. With *Celebrate with Chocolate*, I hope to persuade you that life is a celebration. And, all celebrations deserve chocolate.

EQUIPMENT, INGREDIENTS, AND TECHNIQUES

EQUIPMENT

When I graduated from the Culinary Institute of America in 1965, I never dreamed that I would become a cookbook author. My chef fantasies encompassed a world of impressive kitchens outfitted with eight-burner cooktops, stacked ovens, five-foot-tall stock pots, sparkling stainless steel walls, and many busy hands producing exemplary food. My dream became a reality. I have been working in such kitchens, including the kitchen in my own restaurant, The Trellis, in Williamsburg, Virginia, for more than twenty-five years. I sought additional challenges; owning other restaurants was not a consideration, so when I wrote my first cookbook in 1987, I knew I had found another calling.

When I wrote my first five cookbooks, all the recipe testing was accomplished in the home I share with my wife, Connie. Most cookbook authors I know also work from their home kitchens to make certain that consumers will get the same results as the author promises in his or her book. This can only be accomplished by using the same equipment and by cooking surroundings similar to those found in a typical home kitchen (of course, saying "typical" opens up a rather large bag of flour). Although I enjoyed working in my home kitchen, the constant recipe development and testing was taking its toll on my equipment. So in 1995 my business partner, John Curtis, and I bought a piece of property in James City County, Virginia, located about four miles from The Trellis (and two miles from the historic settlement of Jamestown).

Celebrate with Chocolate is the fourth book I have completed in a 1,600-square-foot building dedicated only to cookbook recipe testing. All of the equipment we use at Ganache Hill—which is what I named the more than one-acre hilltop on which the test kitchen is perched—is found in an average kitchen. The cooktop, ovens, the small appliances such as food processors and electric mixers, and miscellaneous equipment such as baking sheets and bowls, were purchased from local kitchen equipment outlets, department stores, hardware stores, and supermarkets.

Although the following list of equipment is not complete by any means, as many items as possible should be in your kitchen so that you can produce the magical desserts we make at Ganache Hill and in this book.

BAKING SHEETS AND CAKE PANS

All of the baking sheets and cake pans used for testing the recipes in this cookbook were for home rather than professional use. Most were purchased at local Williamsburg stores. The exceptions were the 6 × 3-inch aluminum anodized-finish cake pan for the Just for the Two of Us Birthday Cake, the 6 × 2-inch aluminum anodized-finish cake pans for both the Pretty in Pink Cake and Brett and Kelly's Commitment Cake, and the 4 × 1½-inch nonstick springform pans for the Chocolate Banana Rum Raisin Ice Cream Cakes. (These pans were purchased from Wilton Enterprises at www.wilton.com.) Our baking sheets all have nonstick surfaces and most are 10 × 15 inches. They all have sides for extra rigidity (to prevent them from warping when they are in the oven). Although we always use nonstick baking sheets, we often butter and sometimes line sheets with parchment paper or wax paper to ensure quick release of a baked product, be it cookie or cake. Some batters, especially those with lots of sugar, will stick even to nonstick surfaces. Not only will buttering and papering assist in the effortless release of a product from a pan or baking sheet but will also put a smile on the pot washer's visage, as the task of cleaning will be palliated. I recommend the following manufacturers for quality, value, and accessibility: Ekco Housewares, Inc. (Baker's Secret), Lodge Manufacturing Company (Lodge Cast Iron Cookware), Nordic Ware (Bundt Brand Bakeware), Farberware Inc. (Professional Series), and W. F. Kaiser & Co. (Noblesse Kaiser).

BOWLS

I recommend both stainless steel bowls, which are noncorrosive, and economical glass bowls, also noncorrosive and easy to clean. The stainless steel bowls are better conductors of heat and cold, so use one when setting up an ice-water bath. Glass bowls are necessary for use in a microwave oven. These bowl sizes correspond with those recommended in this book:

small = 1½ to 2 quarts
medium = 2½ to 3 quarts
large = 3½ to 4 quarts
extra large = 6 to 7 quarts

DOUBLE BOILER

At Ganache Hill, we usually nest a stainless steel or glass bowl over a saucepan to fashion a double boiler. When using such a makeshift double boiler, be certain that half of the bowl can be inserted into the saucepan, and that the bowl covers the entire top of the pan. Prior to setting the bowl over the saucepan, place about 1 inch water in the pan. The bottom of the bowl should not touch the water in the pan. The same applies when using a conventional double boiler composed of two saucepans, the top pan nesting perfectly into the bottom. Keeping the bottom of the bowl or top saucepan from contact with the water will prevent chocolate and other foods from getting too hot and scorching.

ELECTRIC MIXERS

To produce the desired volume and most consistent recipe results, I recommend a table-model electric mixer. Buy an extra bowl, which will come in handy for recipes like the Chocolate Madras Cake (page 51). In this recipe, the beating of egg yolks is immediately followed by the whisking of egg whites. Rather than transferring the yolks to a separate bowl, then cleaning the electric mixer bowl before whisking the egg whites, you can simply remove the bowl with the yolks along with the paddle, then insert the extra bowl with a balloon whip. At Ganache Hill, we have two KitchenAid mixers, a model K5SS 5-quart, as well as a model KSM90 4½-quart. I find the pouring shield attachment a necessity for the table-model mixer to keep flour and other ingredients from flying out of the bowl. Handheld electric mixers are effective for many batters, especially if they are small in volume, but these mixers are useless when mixing large amounts of batter or when mixing dense doughs or batters.

If you are serious about successful dessert making, make an investment in a table-model mixer. A quality mixer will give you many years of reliable service.

ICE CREAM MACHINE

Making ice cream at home has become easier in the last few years because of innovative (hands-free and simple to use) and inexpensive (fifty- to sixty-dollar) machines. Previously you could choose an electronically cooled, countertop ice cream freezer with about a 2-quart capacity that would set you back a thousand dollars or so, or a hand-cranked machine that required ice and salt and was tedious to use. Today's easy-to-use electric machines require no cranking, ice, or salt. Just freeze the ice cream in an insulated canister insert that has been frozen for about twenty-four hours, then inserted in the electrically driven base of the machine. With this type of machine, it takes about thirty minutes for the ice cream to be frozen enough to place in the freezer to harden further. Look for a machine that makes from 1½ to 2 quarts in kitchenware and department stores.

ICE WATER BATH

Many home cooks and bakers are not familiar with the ice water bath. This helps to quickly cool hot food so it can be stored in the refrigerator without bacteria growth occurring. Certain foods may be cooled in the refrigerator if handled properly, such as ganache, when spread onto a baking sheet in a thin layer that will cool rapidly in the refrigerator. Other food items, such as hot ice cream custard, need to be cold before they can be transferred to an ice cream machine. Custards are more efficiently cooled by being placed in a 3- to 4-quart bowl, which is then placed in a sink or an extra large bowl (6- to 7-quart) partially filled with ice water. A stainless steel bowl is a better conductor of cold than glass or plastic. Stir the hot mixture frequently for quick cooling.

MICROWAVE OVEN

How things have changed! Since the microwave oven was introduced for home use in the late 1960s until 1999, I was always quick to say that I did not own one—not at home, not at my restaurant. After all, I was a professional chef. Now that I am also a cookbook author, my tune has changed, especially when it comes to melting chocolate in the microwave oven (see pages 20–21). At Ganache Hill we use a Panasonic Model NN-S758, 1100-watt microwave oven that we purchased for the modest price of $150 at our local Target.

The settings vary widely on microwave ovens made by different manufacturers, so I urge caution when following explicit directions such as those listed in Techniques for melting chocolate in a microwave. Use your own oven owner's manual. Just to be on the safe side, I would err in favor of caution the first time and place the chocolate, or whatever else you are heating, on a lower setting than suggested and heat for a few seconds less.

OVENS

I will use the bully pulpit of this cookbook to stress the importance to successful baking of knowing the exact internal temperature of your oven versus the setting. Most ovens, whether they are designed for commercial operation or for the home kitchen, are very unreliable when it comes to the oven temperature settings. Typically, I have found a 20° to 25°F difference between the temperature selected and the actual oven temperature. You may successfully braise meat or even roast a chicken with this temperature variance, but when it comes to cakes, cookies, and other baked goods, forget about it! The only way to ensure that an oven is operating at a designated temperature is to place a mercury-filled tube thermometer in the oven and rely on the thermometer rather than the oven setting, whether manual or digital, for an accurate temperature.

PARCHMENT OR WAX PAPER

The use of parchment (or wax) paper to line cake pans helps ensure that baked cake layers will release effortlessly from the pans. Although it may sound strange that I sometimes call for so-called nonstick pans to be lined with paper and also buttered, I have found this method to work the best with certain recipes. Wax paper may be used as a substitute for parchment paper except in the few cases when the paper is directly exposed to heat (the paraffin on wax paper will melt in the oven if the surface of the paper is exposed—if the paper is not covered with cake batter, for example—or when the rigidity of the parchment paper is preferred over that of wax paper.

PASTRY BAG

I have never been a fan of the traditional canvas pastry bag or even of the easier-to-clean, plastic-lined fabric pastry bag. Cleaning the bags is tedious work, and having those bags staring at me like dunce caps in some nightmare while they were drying out before being stored was strange. I prefer disposable plastic bags. Pipe and toss is where it's at! Check out www.wilton.com for plastic disposable pastry bags.

SAUCEPANS

In my last book, *Death by Chocolate Cakes*, I wrote that "I have never been overly particular about the pedigree of the cookware I own." Then I went on to say that I had recently had a change of heart about cookware because of receiving a piece that was of fine quality as well as beautiful. I opined that perhaps my casual attitude about cookware would change. Well, here we are three years later, and I still have that one outstanding piece of cookware surrounded by the same ragtag saucepans that we have always had at Ganache Hill. If you have the means to purchase the finest cookware available, by all means do so; but such cookware certainly is not critical for the baker or cook, because for the most part, any old pot or pan will do. Below are the saucepan sizes suggested in this book and their equivalents:

small = 1 quart
medium = 1½ to 2 quarts
large = 3 quarts

SPATULAS

OFFSET SPATULA   A spatula with an offset blade is very handy for spreading batter inside cake pans. Although a rubber spatula or an icing spatula will do, the task of spreading within the confines of a cake pan is made easier with an offset spatula. I recommend an offset spatula with a 4- to 5-inch-long and ¾-inch-wide blade.

RUBBER SPATULA   The rubber spatula is one of the most effective tools a baker or cook can have. No other tool is as useful for removing every ounce of batter, chocolate, or other foods from the inside of a mixing bowl or food processor bowl. Keep a selection of rubber spatulas in many sizes on hand along with a few heat resistant spatulas for working with very hot ingredients.

UTILITY TURNER   For the "big jobs" such as transferring one of our not insubstantial cakes from a cardboard cake circle to a serving platter, a spatula known as a utility turner with a blade about 3 inches wide and 7 to 8 inches long will do the trick.

THERMOMETERS

CANDY THERMOMETER At Ganache Hill we use a very precise temperature measuring device for gauging the temperature of items such as bubbling hot sugar and vegetable oil being heated in a deep fryer. Our Taylor glass thermometer housed in a stainless steel jacket accurately measures temperatures from 100° to 400°F.

OVEN THERMOMETER The only way to ensure that an oven is operating at a designated temperature is to place a mercury-filled tube thermometer in the oven and rely on that rather than on the oven setting, whether manual or digital, for an accurate temperature. This type of thermometer may be left in the oven at all times, no matter how high the heat, with the exception of the self-clean setting, which produces heat high enough to ruin most thermometers. These thermometers may be found in hardware stores.

INSTANT-READ THERMOMETER Keep this type of thermometer out of the oven (the protective glass cover is not heat resistant); use it when you need an instant reading of the internal temperature of a cheesecake, or a gauge of how hot or cold a liquid may be. Look for an instant-read thermometer with a range of 0° to 200°F at a variety of retail outlets or online.

WHISKS

How elegant and useful the whisk! Some stiff, others springy, all tactile. A hands-on piece of equipment that is essential for so many kitchen procedures. I suggest a few different sizes of stainless steel whisks from 6 to 12 inches in length, equally divided between light and flexible whisks (for light batters, whipped cream, and meringues), and heavier gauge and sturdy whisks (for sauces, heavy batters, and ganache).

INGREDIENTS

All of the ingredients used for testing the recipes in this book were purchased at local (Williamsburg, Virginia) supermarkets or specialty food stores. This point is made to emphasize that it isn't necessary to reside in a big city to have access to top-notch ingredients and turn out amazing chocolate desserts.

I am an ardent proponent of market shopping. Without high-quality ingredients, a baker is destined to produce second-rate desserts. Even shelf-stable products such as unsweetened cocoa powder will deteriorate if stored in the cupboard for too many moons. Buy what is needed, when it is needed. When purchasing items such as baking soda, spices, chocolate, and other dry goods, look for small containers. Although it may seem more economical to purchase in bulk, when these items start having birthdays, they will not deliver their intended flavor or fulfill their function.

Read the list of ingredients in each recipe and make sure you have all the ingredients on hand before you start. Organize the ingredients as listed in the recipe, which means cut the butter into ½-ounce pieces, chop the chocolate, measure the flour, and don't start production until you have all of the ingredients assembled and in a state of preparedness as described in the ingredient list.

I offer the following information about some of the essential ingredients used throughout this book, as a guide to selecting the specific quality of product needed for the preparation of extraordinary desserts. The brands used at Ganache Hill are listed merely to offer a benchmark for quality product, not as an endorsement.

BAKING POWDER AND BAKING SODA

Baking soda and baking powder are leaveners that are activated as soon as they are added to a liquid. Baking soda (pure bicarbonate of soda) delivers its punch when the liquid is acidic, such as buttermilk; double-acting baking powder (an amalgam of bicarbonate of soda, cream of tartar, and cornstarch) goes on its way no matter the liquid, as the cream of tartar provides the acidity. As soon as the soda or powder is added to a batter, leavening begins. So don't let the batter sit around; get it in the oven right away.

Always check the expiration date on the package (usually found on the bottom), especially with baking powder. This is not to say that past the expiration dates these products will not do their levitating work, but why take the chance? I also recommend purchasing the smallest package of each available. Be precise in the measurement of both these ingredients, as too much or too little will not deliver the desired results.

Finally, please do not use baking soda that has been placed in the fridge for the last few months as an odor suppressor; otherwise, the bicarbonate of soda police will be knocking on your door.

At Ganache Hill we use Calumet baking powder and Arm & Hammer baking soda.

BUTTER

My admiration and love for butter has never wavered. What is it that makes butter so desirable? Butter, whether served at table or used as an ingredient in sweet or savory recipes, brings an inimitable fullness of flavor to food. I would much prefer to eat a very modest portion (even just a single bite) of a pastry made with butter than to indulge in a huge confection that has been produced using a bogus butter-like product.

Butter contributes positively on all fronts when it comes to baked desserts, brownies, or even when the confection is not baked, like truffles. In baked desserts, butter has positive effects on flavor, moistness, crumb texture, and even leavening. When it comes to truffles, butter provides much of their melt-in-your-mouth character.

It is a rare recipe in this book that does not contain butter. At Ganache Hill and The Trellis, we purchase U.S. Grade AA unsalted butter. Unsalted butter should be stored in the refrigerator or freezer to deter rancidity. All of the butter used in these recipes was taken directly from the refrigerator. Unsalted butter should never be kept at room temperature for more than a few hours. Although I prefer the ultra pure taste of unsalted butter, it may turn rancid if not properly stored. If you are not able to purchase unsalted butter, you may use salted butter for the recipes in this book without altering the recipes.

For long-term storage, more than a week or so, I store butter in the freezer. To help prevent rancidity, always thaw frozen butter in the refrigerator rather than at room temperature (this may take a couple of days).

Use softened butter if you choose to use a handheld electric mixer or a whisk, rather than the recommended table-model electric mixer.

At Ganache Hill we use Land O Lakes butter.

CHOCOLATE

CHOCOLATE A HEALTH FOOD? the headline screams in the *New York Times*. Every month, it seems, a university somewhere in America releases

MEASURING BUTTER

These equivalents will make it easy to measure a hard stick of butter just taken from the refrigerator if you don't have a scale:

1 ounce	=	2 tablespoons	=	¼ stick
2 ounces	=	4 tablespoons	=	½ stick
3 ounces	=	6 tablespoons		
5 ounces	=	10 tablespoons		
6 ounces	=	12 tablespoons	=	1½ sticks
¼ pound	=	8 tablespoons	=	1 stick

For chopped butter:

¼ ounce	=	½ tablespoon

For melted butter used in pan preparation:

1 teaspoon = ⅓ tablespoon

the results of a study on the wholesomeness of chocolate. The latest excitement centers around flavonoids, which are powerful antioxidants. I wish these university researchers would realize that most people do not need to be encouraged to partake of the fruit of the cacao tree. The fact is that most people are already passionate about eating chocolate (the ones I know, anyway). Although I shall never be mistaken for a university researcher, it is my hope that the research underlying this cookbook will encourage you to eat chocolate not only for its healthful effects but for the sheer joy it will bring when consumed.

Ganache Hill test kitchen chef Brett Bailey purchased all of the chocolate used to test the recipes in this book at local (Williamsburg, Virginia) supermarkets. Fortunately, several excellent chocolate manu facturers produce high-quality chocolate here in the United States. All of the brands we purchased will be familiar to the home baker and are available at most supermarkets. Although I find certain brands of European chocolate to be delicious, some are too complex and deliver flavors that may be overwhelming and bitter to some. Whether you purchase chocolate manufactured in the United States or in Europe, I encourage you to read the ingredient list on the back to verify that you are purchasing real chocolate. If the label lists any fat other than cocoa butter, it's not bona fide. Some manufacturers add palm kernel oil and/or coconut oil to their chocolates. Give those chocolates a wide berth.

Although the experts recommend that storage conditions for chocolate be cool and dry (at a temperature range of 65° to 68°F with 50 percent relative humidity), I have found that an air-conditioned room temperature in the range of 68° to 78°F works fine. If storage conditions are too warm, the chocolate may develop gray surface streaks caused by the cocoa butter in the chocolate rising to the surface, and when conditions are damp, the sugar may possibly do the same thing. If you purchase only what you need for a particular recipe, you should not have to concern yourself with storage conditions.

TYPES OF CHOCOLATE

CHOCOLATE CHIPS AND MINI-MORSELS Use chips and mini-morsels only when a recipe calls for them. Never substitute chips or mini-morsels in recipes calling for semisweet baking chocolate. Although pleasing to eat out of hand and deliciously textural in chocolate chip cookies and other recipes, chips and mini-morsels are not—I repeat, not—suitable as a substitute for baking chocolate. Most chips and morsels are formulated differently from baking chocolate, which is the reason they maintain their shape even after being baked. As with other chocolate, choose only chips and mini-morsels that have cocoa butter as the only fat, not palm and/or coconut oil.

At Ganache Hill we use Baker's® Semi-Sweet Real Chocolate Chips and Nestlé Real Semi-Sweet Chocolate Mini Morsels.

MILK CHOCOLATE We use very little milk chocolate in this book—1 ounce for the Chocolate Hazelnut Christmas Tree Stump (page 29)—so little that it seems frivolous to mention it in this section. So I will merely say that if you want a bar of milk chocolate suitable for our recipes and delicious eaten out of hand, select the same brand we use.

At Ganache Hill we use Ghirardelli Pure Milk Chocolate.

UNSWEETENED BAKING CHOCOLATE Unsweetened baking chocolate, sometimes called chocolate liquor, is the juice that is produced when roasted cocoa beans are processed, then ground into liquid. After additional processing to ensure smoothness, the liquid is shaped and hardened into blocks. The package labeling for unsweetened chocolate should list only one ingredient—chocolate. Unsweetened chocolate is not eaten on its own, but it is the core of other baking chocolates such as semisweet. Unsweetened chocolate is by composition more than 50 percent cocoa butter; the remaining amount is termed cocoa solids. It contains no sugar or other additives. At Ganache Hill we use Baker's® Unsweetened Baking Chocolate Squares.

SEMISWEET BAKING CHOCOLATE   Semisweet baking chocolate is made up of unsweetened chocolate (a minimum of 35 percent), cocoa butter, sugar, soy lecithin (an emulsifier that keeps the chocolate smooth and liquid), and vanilla extract. Many of the recipes in this book contain some semisweet baking chocolate. If you prefer darker, more assertively flavored chocolate, substitute bittersweet chocolate in exactly the same amount in any of our recipes. As previously mentioned, do not purchase chocolate that contains any fat other than cocoa butter. At Ganache Hill we use Baker's® Semi-Sweet Baking Chocolate Squares.

WHITE CHOCOLATE   Let the buyer beware when it comes to white chocolate. The ingredient listing on a package of white chocolate should be: sugar, cocoa butter, milk, soy lecithin, vanilla extract. Do not buy any white chocolate that lists palm kernel oil and/or coconut oil as ingredients. We found the white chocolate listed below delivered the sought-after results 100 percent of the time when testing recipes in this book that contain white chocolate. I emphasize this not to sell you on the brand but to guarantee success. I get many comments about failed recipes from folks who have purchased imitation white chocolate; i.e., chocolate that did not contain cocoa butter. At Ganache Hill we use Baker's® Premium White Chocolate Baking Squares.

UNSWEETENED COCOA POWDER   The intense chocolate flavor achieved in a recipe with unsweetened cocoa powder is due to the low fat content of the cocoa. Cocoa is produced by hydraulically pressing unsweetened chocolate (which contains 50 to 56 percent cocoa butter) to remove most of the cocoa butter. Cocoa, however, is not totally fat free; it does contain residual amounts of cocoa butter. The lack of cocoa butter makes cocoa highly soluble in liquid—think hot chocolate. The flavor intensity of cocoa is diminished by exposure to air, so purchase small containers and keep the container tightly sealed. Look at the container closely before purchasing to make certain you are not selecting a breakfast cocoa drink mix. The only ingredient listed on the package should be cocoa. At Ganache Hill we use Hershey's Cocoa.

CREAM

Heavy cream, a.k.a. whipping cream, is luscious and luxurious on the palate, somewhat like a butterfly alighting on a stamen. Ever so delicate in flavor, yet almost overwhelming in how it feels in the mouth, cream, when in concert with chocolate, comes together as the confectionery miracle known as ganache. Of course, it does much more, as can be witnessed by the inclusion of cream in a majority of the recipes in this cookbook.

Unless you have a milk cow grazing in your backyard, you will probably have to settle for purchasing ultra pasteurized cream rather than fresh. All of the recipes in this cookbook were tested using ultra pasteurized cream purchased at the supermarket.

One big advantage ultra pasteurized cream has over fresh is its long shelf life; it will stay fresh under refrigeration for weeks. On the ever-so-slight downside, ultra pasteurized cream does not burst forth with pure flavor as does fresh cream. When used as a dessert ingredient, however, ultra pasteurized cream is almost impossible to distinguish from fresh. At Ganache Hill we use Richfood® Heavy Whipping Cream.

EGGS

Without getting into a chemistry lesson, suffice it to say that eggs are a natural as well as culinary phenomenon. When cooking with eggs they must be fresh. If you are as scientifically challenged as I am, that's about all you need to know about the egg (I myself was never intrigued by the which came first theory).

Fresh Grade AA large eggs are essential for the successful preparation of recipes in this cookbook. Always purchase eggs from a refrigerated display case, and get them back into refrigeration as soon as possible. Using smaller or larger size eggs may have a negative impact on most recipes in this cookbook. Although the substitution of one size egg for another may sometimes work, I can't guarantee that it will. I have not found that room temperature egg whites whisk up into more volume than refrigerated egg whites (in all of our recipe testing we use refrigerated egg whites). To stay healthy, avoid consuming raw eggs (keep your fingers out of the batter). At Ganache Hill we use U.S. Grade AA large eggs from the supermarket.

FLOUR

All of the measurements for flour in this cookbook are presifted, so measure, then sift. Using a quality brand of flour such as Gold Medal makes sense to me (although some lesser known regional brands such as White Lily are exceptional), especially with so little pricing difference between branded and generic. Improperly milled flour can substantially affect the quality of a pastry. Always make certain that the flour specified is what you are using; in other words, don't substitute cake flour for all-purpose. At Ganache Hill we use Gold Medal® all-purpose flour and Swans Down® cake flour.

TECHNIQUES

I have made an effort to include as much technique information as possible in each recipe, and, if not there, then in the Chef's Touch of each recipe. Perhaps one of the most useful techniques is the organization of the ingredients. Another point, though perhaps not a technique *per se*, is the thorough reading of a recipe before getting started. The recipe is your road map to success. Closely followed, it will lead to a destination of delectation. Disregarding the recipe may lead to a bumpy road with confectionery mishaps. Here are some additional techniques to point you in the direction of pleasurable progress.

MAKING CHOCOLATE CURLS

Easily fashioned chocolate curls with their distinctive appearance add a special finishing touch. In Rolf's Old-World Black Forest Cake (page 42), 2 ounces of semisweet chocolate curls are needed to garnish the cake. Although this is accurate, you will have to start making the curls from a piece of chocolate larger than 2 ounces; otherwise, you will have shavings, rather than large curls. An 8-ounce or so block of chocolate is just about the right size (larger is fine, smaller is torture). It helps if the chocolate is at warm room temperature, 82°F or so, rather than at cool air-conditioned room temperature, 72°F or less. Use a sharp vegetable peeler to shave curls from the block. Chocolate curls may be prepared in advance, then stored in a tightly sealed plastic container in the refrigerator until needed.

MELTING CHOCOLATE IN A DOUBLE BOILER

Although using a double boiler to melt chocolate is simple and efficient, we now use the even simpler and very efficient microwave oven to melt chocolate at Ganache Hill. If you choose the double boiler method, some precautions should be noted: First set up the double boiler as described in the Equipment section (see page 8). Melt coarsely chopped chocolate slowly over medium-low or medium heat while stirring frequently with a rubber spatula until the chocolate is completely melted and smooth. Melting too quickly over high heat may render scorched, inedible chocolate. Avoid introducing any moisture into the melting or already melted chocolate; otherwise, it may seize (the chocolate stiffens into an unusable, coagulated mass). Once melted, the chocolate should stay fluid for 30 to 60 minutes, depending upon the temperature in your kitchen. If your kitchen is cool, keep the melted chocolate over warm water until ready to use, unless the recipe requires the chocolate to be chilled before using.

AMOUNT OF CHOPPED CHOCOLATE	APPROXIMATE MELTING TIME
1 to 2 ounces	2½ to 3 minutes
3 to 4 ounces	3½ to 4 minutes
5 to 6 ounces	4½ to 5 minutes
7 to 8 ounces	5½ to 6 minutes
9 to 16 ounces	6½ to 8 minutes

MELTING CHOCOLATE IN A MICROWAVE OVEN

Microwave coarsely chopped chocolate in a glass bowl. After removing the chocolate from the microwave oven, use a rubber spatula to stir until smooth. There seems to be no uniformity in microwave oven power settings. At Ganache Hill, we use an 1100-watt microwave oven on the medium setting for melting chocolate. The following melting times may vary depending on the model, wattage, and power settings on your microwave oven.

AMOUNT OF CHOPPED CHOCOLATE	APPROXIMATE MELTING TIME
1 to 3 ounces	1½ minutes
4 to 8 ounces	2 to 2½ minutes
9 to 16 ounces	2½ to 3 minutes

MELTING CHOCOLATE WITH OTHER INGREDIENTS

Several of the recipes in this cookbook require melting chopped chocolate with other ingredients such as butter and cream. As with melting chocolate by itself, a modicum of attention and care is recommended. It's always best to heat chocolate slower rather than faster, and over lower rather than higher heat. If it seems odd that in some cases it takes less time to melt chocolate with other ingredients in the microwave oven than chocolate by itself, that is because the fat in butter and cream attracts the microwaves and accelerates the cooking process.

AMOUNT OF INGREDIENTS	DOUBLE BOILER TIME	MICROWAVE OVEN TIME
2 ounces semisweet chocolate and 1 ounce unsweetened chocolate with 3 ounces unsalted butter	1½ minutes	5½ to 6 minutes
4 ounces semisweet chocolate with 2 ounces unsalted butter	1¾ minutes	5 to 5½ minutes
3 ounces semisweet chocolate and 2 ounces unsweetened chocolate with 2 ounces unsalted butter	1¾ minutes	6½ to 7 minutes

AMOUNT OF INGREDIENTS	DOUBLE BOILER TIME	MICROWAVE OVEN TIME
4 ounces semisweet chocolate and 4 ounces unsweetened chocolate with ¼ pound (1 stick) unsalted butter	2½ minutes	6½ to 7 minutes
6 ounces white chocolate with ½ cup half-and-half	2 minutes	6 to 6½ minutes
6 ounces semisweet chocolate and 2 ounces unsweetened chocolate with ¼ pound (1 stick) unsalted butter	2 minutes	6½ to 7 minutes
8 ounces semisweet chocolate with ½ pound (2 sticks) unsalted butter	2 minutes	6½ to 7 minutes
12 ounces semisweet chocolate with ¼ cup heavy cream and 5 ounces unsalted butter	2¾ minutes	7 to 7½ minutes
1 pound semisweet chocolate and 3 ounces unsweetened chocolate with ¼ pound (1 stick) unsalted butter	3 minutes	8½ to 9 minutes

SIFTING DRY INGREDIENTS

Sifting dry baking ingredients such as flour and cocoa breaks up any lumps and eliminates foreign objects. Sifting also aerates the ingredients, making them easier to incorporate into the first stages of a batter, contributing to a smoother batter. Sift dry ingredients onto a large piece of parchment paper (or wax paper) to make them easier to pick up and add to a mixing bowl.

SKINNING HAZELNUTS

Skinned hazelnuts seem to be readily available in most supermarkets. If you are not able to purchase skinned hazelnuts, toast the hazelnuts on a baking sheet with sides in a preheated 325°F oven for 18 minutes. Remove the nuts from the oven and immediately cover with a damp cotton towel large enough to drape over the entire top of the baking sheet. Invert another baking sheet with sides over the other sheet to hold in the steam and make the nuts easier to skin. After 5 minutes, remove the skins from the nuts by placing them inside a folded dry cotton kitchen towel and rubbing vigorously.

TOASTING NUTS

Always purchase unsalted nuts. I prefer purchasing whole shelled nuts when available, or shelled nut halves rather than nut pieces, because I think the quality of the nuts is superior when whole or halved rather than chopped. Since nuts are perishable, I recommend storing them in the refrigerator or freezer (refrigerated or frozen nuts should be brought to room temperature before toasting and using). Toasting nuts accentuates their flavor and dissipates any moisture the absorbent nut flesh may have acquired during storage. We toasted all the nuts (with the exception of dry roasted peanuts) before using them in the recipes in this book. Once toasted, nuts should be completely cooled before chopping, especially if chopping is done in a food processor; otherwise, the nuts may end up as a nut butter rather than as discernable chopped pieces. Sometimes I recommend chopping nuts with a knife, rather than using a food processor when a particular size is desired.

For best results toast nuts at 325°F.

NUT	TOASTING TIME
pecan halves	12 minutes
pine nuts	8 minutes
skinned hazelnuts	12 minutes
sliced almonds	10 minutes
unsalted macadamia nuts	18 minutes
walnut halves	14 minutes
whole cashews	12 minutes

CAKES

When it comes to celebrating, nothing beats cake.
This delightful assortment comes in all shapes and
sizes, from a birthday cake for two with a
stick-to-the-lips meringue icing, to a cranberry
topped extravaganza that will tantalize the eyes
as well as the palate.

Brett and Kelly's Commitment Cake

When planning their outdoor wedding in September 1996 in the Finger Lakes region of New York, Brett and Kelly Bailey (Ganache Hill test kitchen chef and Trellis pastry chef) knew they wanted a cake with a lusty chocolaty center covered with an appealing buttercream. With this in mind, Kelly designed a cake that not only made a stunning presentation but ensured an eating experience in synch with their professional passions.

Of all the traditions of the nuptial day, saving the top tier of the cake for the betrothed to consume on their first anniversary should be rethought. No cake is enhanced by spending twelve months in the deep freeze. It is no wonder that so many couples haul it out more as a symbol than as a magical reprise of lips smeared with buttercream, whispering promises soon to be requited.

Kelly offers this recipe for Maple Almond Buttercream–coated Cocoa Honey Cake for just the top tier of the Bailey wedding cake, hoping to initiate a tradition of an annual commitment cake for renewing pledges of love, happiness, and great chocolate.

MAKE THE COCOA HONEY CAKE   Preheat the oven to 325°F.

Lightly coat the insides of two 6 × 2-inch aluminum cake pans with the melted butter. Flour the insides of the pans with the 2 teaspoons flour. Shake out any excess flour. Set aside.

In a sifter combine the ¾ cup flour, the cocoa powder, baking powder, and baking soda. Sift directly into the bowl of an electric mixer. Position the bowl on an electric mixer fitted with a paddle. Add the ¼ pound butter and the sugar. Mix on low speed for 2 minutes, until the butter is cut into the dry ingredients and the mixture develops a granular texture similar to that of a pie or tart dough. Turn the mixer off.

Heat the clover honey, milk, and water in a small saucepan over

COCOA HONEY CAKE

2 teaspoons unsalted butter, melted

¼ pound (1 stick) unsalted butter, cut into ½-ounce pieces

¾ cup all-purpose flour plus 2 teaspoons

¼ cup unsweetened cocoa powder

½ teaspoon baking powder

¼ teaspoon baking soda

¼ cup granulated sugar

¼ cup clover honey

¼ cup whole milk

¼ cup water

1 large egg

MAPLE ALMOND BUTTERCREAM

½ pound (2 sticks) unsalted butter, cut into ½-ounce pieces

¼ cup 100% pure U.S. Grade A dark amber maple syrup

¼ teaspoon pure almond extract

½ cup granulated sugar

2 large egg whites

¼ cup sliced almonds,
   toasted (see page 23)
Assortment of fresh, edible
   flowers

SERVES 2

medium heat. Bring to a simmer, then remove from the heat. Immediately add the egg and whisk to incorporate. Add the very hot mixture to the dough in the mixing bowl and mix on low speed to incorporate, about 30 seconds. Remove the bowl from the mixer and finish mixing the batter by hand with a rubber spatula.

Immediately divide the cake batter into the prepared pans (about 1 cup of batter in each pan), using a rubber spatula to transfer all of the batter into the pans (the batter is liquid enough to make the usual step of "spreading evenly" unnecessary). Bake on the center rack of the oven until a toothpick inserted in the center of each cake layer comes out clean, 24 to 25 minutes. Remove the cake layers from the oven and cool in the pans for 15 minutes at room temperature. Invert the cake layers onto cake circles wrapped with plastic wrap or lined with parchment paper (or invert onto cake plates). Immediately turn the cake layers over again, top side up, onto circles or plates. Refrigerate.

MAKE THE MAPLE ALMOND BUTTERCREAM   Place the butter in the bowl of an electric mixer fitted with a paddle. Mix on low speed for 1 minute, then increase the speed to medium-high and beat for 2 minutes until soft. Scrape down the sides of the bowl and the paddle. Beat on medium for 2 more minutes until very soft. Operate the mixer on medium while gradually adding the maple syrup; mix until thoroughly incorporated, about 2 minutes. Add the almond extract and beat on medium for 20 seconds. Unless you have another mixing bowl for your electric mixer, transfer the maple- and almond-enhanced butter to a medium bowl and set aside at room temperature.

Heat 1 inch of water in a large saucepan over medium heat. When the water begins to simmer, place the sugar and egg whites in a large bowl. Set the bowl into the saucepan (the bottom of the bowl should not touch the water). Using a handheld whisk, gently whisk the sugar and egg whites until the mixture reaches a temperature of 140°F, 4 to 4½ minutes.

Transfer the heated egg white mixture to the bowl of an electric mixer fitted with a balloon whip. (The bowl and whip must be meticulously clean and dry; otherwise, the egg white mixture will not whisk properly.) Whisk on high until the temperature of the egg white mixture has been reduced to about 82°F, about 5 minutes. If the temperature is much warmer than that, the butter may melt when added in the next step. Add half of the maple- and almond-enhanced whipped butter to the egg whites and whisk on high for 30 seconds. Add the remaining butter to the mixing bowl and whisk on high for 30 seconds. Scrape down the sides of the bowl and the paddle. Whisk on high for 15 more seconds. Transfer ½ cup buttercream to a pastry bag fitted with a small straight tip.

ASSEMBLE THE CAKE   Remove the cake layers from the refrigerator. Use a cake spatula to evenly and smoothly spread ½ cup of buttercream over the top and to the edges of one of the cake layers. Place the second cake layer onto the buttercream-coated cake layer and gently press into place. Evenly and smoothly spread the remaining buttercream onto the top and sides of the cake; refrigerate the cake for 15 minutes.

Use a utility turner (wide spatula) to transfer the cake to a serving platter. Gently press individual almond slices, lengthwise, into the buttercream around the base of the cake, with the slices touching. Pipe a border of ⅜-inch beads of buttercream next to the almond slices around the base of the cake, with the beads touching. Use a 2¾-inch ring mold (or a thin-lipped glass of the same size) to gently press an outline in the center of the top of the cake. Using the outline as a guide, gently press individual almond slices into the buttercream around the outline (the tips of the almonds should be about 1 inch away from the outside edge of the top of the cake). Pipe a ring of ⅜-inch beads of buttercream along the inside of the ring of almonds, with the beads touching. Refrigerate until needed.

TO SERVE   Remove the cake from the refrigerator an hour before your celebration. Decorate the top center of the cake, inside the buttercream bead border, with fresh edible flowers. Heat the blade of a serrated slicer under hot running water and wipe the blade dry before making each slice. Serve immediately.

𝒯HE CHEF'S TOUCH

If you don't have 6 × 2-inch aluminum cake pans in your equipment cupboard, check with a specialty kitchenware store, or order online from Wilton Enterprises at www.wilton.com.

Take the time to scrutinize the label when choosing maple syrup.

Many choices, even though they claim to be 100% pure and Grade A, are of substandard quality. For the best, that is, most maple sugary and pure in flavor, select 100% pure U.S. Grade A dark amber maple syrup. I am particularly fond of Vermont and Pennsylvania products.

Flowers provide a visual foil to the striking perfection of the cake. Ask your florist for assistance in selecting an appropriate edible flower or array of flowers to garnish the cake.

This cake may be prepared over 2 days.

DAY 1: Bake the Cocoa Honey Cake. Once its cooled, cover with plastic wrap and refrigerate.

DAY 2: Prepare the Maple Almond Buttercream. Assemble Brett and Kelly's Commitment Cake and serve as directed in the recipe.

After assembly, keep the cake (with the exception of the floral garnish) in the refrigerator for 2 to 3 days before serving. To avoid permeating the cake with refrigerator odors, place it in a large, tightly sealed plastic container.

Chocolate Hazelnut Christmas Tree Stump

The traditional French Christmas cake known as *bûche de Noël* may have been conceived as a whimsical confectionery take on the centuries-old custom of burning a log to usher in the Christmas season. In Williamsburg, Virginia, a *bûche de Noël* is often the star of the dessert table. At a supper given for Governor and Mrs. A. Linwood Holton at Carter's Grove, an eighteenth-century plantation, on December 18, 1971, *bûche de Noël* was the centerpiece of a dessert table that was shared with fresh fruit, wine jelly with custard sauce, sweetmeats, and toasted pecans. Unlike the usual horizontal log with one rolled layer, this stump cake has more than 3 rings of cake. It is 3 cakes, cut into 6 strips, and when rolled and cut it makes 10 to 12 rings with dark chocolate icing, which makes it look like a stump rather than a small log.

MAKE THE TRIPLE CHOCOLATE HAZELNUT BARK Line a 10 × 15-inch baking sheet with sides with a 12 × 16-inch piece of parchment paper (or wax paper).

Pour the semisweet chocolate onto the paper-lined baking sheet and use an offset spatula to spread it as thinly as possible to the edges of the baking sheet. Using a teaspoon, drizzle the milk chocolate in a herky-jerky fashion over the surface of the semisweet chocolate, then do the same thing with the white chocolate. Use the end of a toothpick to swirl the three chocolates into each other, creating a kaleidoscopic effect. Sprinkle the hazelnuts over the surface of the chocolate. Use the palms of your hands to gently press the nuts into the chocolate. Cover the top of the baking sheet with plastic wrap and place in the freezer.

MAKE THE WHIPPED DARK CHOCOLATE ICING Place the butter in the bowl of an electric mixer fitted with a paddle. Mix on low speed for 1 minute; increase the speed to medium-high and beat for 2 minutes

TRIPLE CHOCOLATE HAZELNUT BARK

8 ounces semisweet baking chocolate, coarsely chopped and melted (see pages 20–21)

1 ounce milk chocolate, coarsely chopped and melted

1 ounce white chocolate, coarsely chopped and melted

1/2 cup skinned hazelnuts, toasted (see page 23) and coarsely chopped

WHIPPED DARK CHOCOLATE ICING

1 pound (4 sticks) unsalted butter, cut into 1/4-ounce pieces

6 ounces unsweetened baking chocolate, coarsely chopped and melted (see pages 20–21)

4 ounces semisweet baking chocolate, coarsely chopped and melted

1 pound confectioners'
   sugar, sifted onto a large
   piece of parchment paper
   (or wax paper)

TOASTED HAZELNUT SPONGE
CAKE

1 tablespoon unsalted
   butter, melted

1 cup cake flour

½ teaspoon baking powder

¼ teaspoon salt

1 cup granulated sugar

7 large eggs, separated

2 tablespoons Frangelico
   (hazelnut-flavored
   liqueur)

1 cup skinned hazelnuts,
   toasted (see page 23) and
   finely chopped

3 tablespoons confectioners'
   sugar

CHOCOLATE RINGS OF TIME

1 ounce semisweet baking
   chocolate, coarsely
   chopped and melted
   (see pages 20–21)

SERVES 10

until soft. Use a rubber spatula to scrape down the sides of the bowl and the paddle. Beat on medium for 2 more minutes until very soft. Scrape down the sides of the bowl and paddle. Add the unsweetened and semi-sweet chocolate and beat on medium for 30 seconds. Scrape down the sides of the bowl and the paddle. Now beat on medium for 15 more seconds. Gradually add the confectioners' sugar while mixing on the lowest speed (stir) until combined, about 1½ minutes. Scrape down the sides of the bowl and the paddle. Beat on medium for 1 more minute until very soft and fluffy. Remove the bowl from the mixer and use a rubber spatula to finish mixing the icing until thoroughly combined. Cover with plastic wrap and set aside at room temperature until needed.

MAKE THE TOASTED HAZELNUT SPONGE CAKE AND ASSEM-BLE THE STUMP   Preheat the oven to 325°F.

Lightly coat three 15 × 10-inch baking sheets with sides with some of the melted butter. Line the bottoms of the sheets with parchment paper (or wax paper), then lightly coat the paper with more melted butter. Set aside.

In a sifter combine the cake flour, baking powder, and salt. Sift onto a large piece of parchment paper (or wax paper) and set aside until needed.

Place ⅔ cup of the granulated sugar, the egg yolks, and the Frangelico in the bowl of an electric mixer fitted with a paddle. Beat on medium-high speed for 4 minutes until the mixture is pale in color and slightly thickened, and the sugar is almost completely dissolved. (Rub a minuscule amount of the batter between your thumb and index finger; the batter should feel pretty smooth with very little grittiness. Don't lick your fingers, however—though the batter may look appealing, it contains raw egg yolks.) Operate the mixer on low while gradually adding the dry ingredients; mix until incorporated, about 45 seconds. Scrape down the sides of the bowl. Beat on medium for 15 more seconds, until thick and well combined. Transfer the mixture into an extra large bowl and set aside while whisking the egg whites.

Place the egg whites and the remaining ⅓ cup granulated sugar in the bowl of an electric mixer fitted with a balloon whip. (Make certain that the bowl and whip are meticulously clean and dry; otherwise the egg white mixture will not whisk properly). Whisk the egg whites and sugar on high speed for 2 minutes, or until stiff peaks form. Remove the bowl from the mixer. Add the hazelnuts, and use a rubber spatula to fold them into the egg whites. Transfer to the egg yolk mixture, and use a rubber spatula to quickly fold in the whites until the mixture has a uniform color. Immediately divide the cake batter into the prepared baking sheets (about 2¼ cups batter in each baking sheet), spreading the batter evenly to the edges (I recommend an offset spatula for easy spreading). Don't worry that the layer of batter is quite thin. The eggs will leaven the batter and supply the right amount of volume. Place the baking sheets on the top, center, and bottom racks of the oven and bake for 9 to 10 minutes—rotate the baking sheets from top to bottom and turn each sheet 180 degrees about halfway through the baking time—until a toothpick inserted into the center of the cake comes out almost clean (because of the stickiness of the batter, the toothpick will not be 100 percent dry), and the edges of the cake start to pull away from the sides of the pan.

While the cakes are baking, sprinkle three 12 × 18-inch pieces of parchment paper (or wax paper) with 1 tablespoon confectioners' sugar each (this prevents the very sticky cakes from adhering to the paper).

Remove the cakes from the oven and immediately invert them onto the sprinkled paper. If the edges of the cakes have not pulled away completely from the sides of the baking sheets, use a sharp, thin-bladed paring knife to carefully cut the cakes away from the sides. Gently peel the paper away from the bottoms of the cakes and discard. Place another 12 × 20 inch piece of paper over the cakes (the side facing up now), and invert the cake again so the baked top is facing up. Remove the top piece of parchment paper (or wax paper) and discard. Spread 1¼ cups of the whipped chocolate icing in a thin layer to the edges of each of the cake layers. Use a sharp knife to cut each of the cakes lengthwise into 2 pieces, yielding six 5 × 15-inch pieces. Begin rolling the stump by starting with the narrow side (i.e., the 5-inch-wide side) nearest you; roll one of the cakes away from you, using the paper to help lift the cake over onto itself. Continue to roll the cake to the opposite end, making a tight roll. Roll the remaining strips of cake, one at a time, around the first roll, making as tight a roll as possible. Transfer this rolled cake, one of the flat sides down, onto a cake circle (or directly onto a cake plate). Spread the remaining icing over the top and down the sides of the cake (try spreading the icing a touch lop-sided on the top to create a small angle to the stump).

Remove the bark from the freezer. Use your hands to break it up into random pieces ½ to 1½ inches in diameter.

Gently press the pieces onto the sides of the cake until the sides are covered (visualize constructing a puzzle). It is fine if the bark pieces overlap. Now the cake resembles a stump covered with bark! There may be a tiny bit of bark left over—go for it, chocolate lover!

APPLY THE CHOCOLATE RINGS OF TIME   Place the semisweet chocolate in a small plastic zippered bag. Snip the tip from a bottom corner of the bag. Pipe a continuous spiral of chocolate onto the top of the stump, starting in the center and slowly working your way toward the edge. Refrigerate the cake for at least 2 hours before cutting.

TO SERVE   Heat the blade of a serrated slicer under hot running water and wipe the blade dry before cutting each slice. (If any of the bark falls away during the cutting, simply stick it back in place, as it will adhere to the icing.) Serve immediately.

𝒯HE CHEF'S TOUCH

The Toasted Hazelnut Sponge Cake is somewhat of a hybrid in that similar to its European cousin, génoise, it contains butter and, unlike most traditional sponge cakes leavened only with eggs, gets a little leavening assistance from ½ teaspoon of baking powder. Hey, that is what being an iconoclast is all about—breaking the rules!

The smooth-flavored Frangelico, produced in Italy, is worth the extra cost. Buy it instead of the harsher, generic hazelnut-flavored liqueurs.

The Triple Chocolate Hazelnut Bark may be prepared and then held in the freezer for up to several days. However, the rest of the cake should be made at the same time, and the cakes should be iced within minutes of being taken from the oven. If the cakes are allowed to cool before being iced, they will be impossible to roll and assemble.

Clear the decks for this recipe. It will facilitate the assembly of the stump if you have plenty of counter space when removing, icing, cutting, then rolling the cakes into a stump.

After assembly, keep the cake in the refrigerator for 2 to 3 days before serving. To avoid permeating the cake with refrigerator odors, place it in a large, tightly sealed plastic container.

PRETTY IN PINK CAKE

Pretty in Pink's promise is a snappy schnapps-flavored chocolate cake paired with strawberry preserves–infused cream cheese icing. My hope is that the seemingly uncomplicated nature of the Pretty in Pink Cake will not make it seem mundane. This is a dessert that can easily find friends at a picnic or an elegant dinner. Not only will its height impress, but the commingling of chocolate and berries will bring plenty of pleasure to the palate.

MAKE THE SCHNAPPY CHOCOLATE CAKE   Preheat the oven to 350°F.

Lightly coat the insides of three 6 × 2-inch aluminum cake pans, using the melted butter. Flour the insides of each pan with 1 teaspoon flour. Shake out and discard the excess flour. Set aside until needed.

Melt the chopped semisweet chocolate and the 2 ounces butter in the top half of a double boiler, or in a small glass bowl in a microwave oven (see pages 20–21) and stir until smooth.

In a sifter combine the ¾ cup flour, the cocoa powder, baking powder, and salt. Sift onto a large piece of parchment paper (or wax paper) and set aside.

Place the granulated sugar and the eggs in the bowl of an electric mixer fitted with a paddle. Beat on medium-high speed for 3 minutes until the mixture is frothy and slightly thickened. Add the chocolate and butter mixture and mix on medium to combine, about 15 seconds. Use a rubber spatula to scrape down the sides of the bowl. Operate the mixer on low while gradually adding the dry ingredients; mix until incorporated, about 45 seconds. Add the schnapps and mix on low for 10 seconds. Remove the bowl from the mixer and use a rubber spatula to finish mixing the ingredients until thoroughly combined (this dense, delectable batter is for your eyes only—no tasting, not yet). Immediately divide the cake batter among the prepared pans (about ⅔ cup of batter in each pan) and spread evenly (the batter is very thick, so this will take a bit of spreading).

SCHNAPPY CHOCOLATE CAKE

2 teaspoons unsalted butter, melted

2 ounces (½ stick) unsalted butter, cut into ½-ounce pieces

¾ cup all-purpose flour plus 3 teaspoons

4 ounces semisweet baking chocolate, coarsely chopped

¼ cup unsweetened cocoa powder

1 teaspoon baking powder

¼ teaspoon salt

½ cup granulated sugar

3 large eggs

1 tablespoon Wilderberry schnapps

PRETTY IN PINK ICING

2 cups confectioners' sugar

½ pound (2 sticks) unsalted
butter, cut into ½-ounce
pieces

6 ounces cream cheese, cut
into 1-ounce pieces

½ cup strawberry preserves

4 to 5 drops red food color

SERVES 4

Bake on the center rack of the oven until a toothpick inserted into the center of each cake layer comes out clean, 15 to 16 minutes. Remove the cake layers from the oven and cool in the pans for 15 minutes at room temperature. Invert the cake layers onto cake circles (or directly onto cake plates), then immediately turn the cake layers baked side up again. Refrigerate the layers.

MAKE THE PRETTY IN PINK ICING Sift the confectioners' sugar onto a large piece of parchment paper (or wax paper). Set aside.

Place the butter in the bowl of an electric mixer fitted with a paddle. Mix on low speed for 1 minute; increase the speed to medium and beat for 2 minutes until soft. Scrape down the sides of the bowl and the paddle. Beat on medium for another 2 minutes until very soft. Add the confectioners' sugar and mix on the lowest speed (stir) to combine, about 1 minute. Scrape down the sides of the bowl and the paddle. Now beat on medium for 10 seconds. Transfer the butter and sugar mixture to a small bowl.

Place the cream cheese in the bowl of an electric mixer fitted with a paddle. Mix on low speed for 1 minute, then increase the speed to medium and beat for 2 minutes until soft. Scrape down the sides of the bowl and the paddle. Beat on medium for another 2 minutes until very soft. Scrape down the sides of the bowl and the paddle. Add the strawberry preserves and beat on medium for 1 minute. Scrape down the sides of the bowl. Add the butter and sugar mixture and beat on medium for 10 seconds. Add the food color (are you in the pink?) and beat for 15 seconds.

ASSEMBLE THE CAKE Remove 2 of the chocolate cake layers from the refrigerator. Use a cake spatula to spread ¾ cup of icing evenly and smoothly over the top and to the edges of each of the cake layers (about ¾ cup of icing for each layer). Refrigerate the iced layers and the remaining icing for 30 minutes. Remove all the cake layers and the icing from the refrigerator. Stack the iced layers, then top with the remaining cake layer. Gently press the layers into place. Spread the remaining icing over the top and sides of the entire cake. Refrigerate the cake for 1 hour before cutting and serving.

TO SERVE Heat the blade of a serrated slicer under hot running water and wipe the blade dry before cutting each slice. Keep the slices at room temperature for 15 to 20 minutes before serving.

*T*HE CHEF'S TOUCH

The 6 × 2-inch aluminum cake pans used in this recipe are available from Wilton Enterprises online at www.wilton.com.

Not pink enough for you? How about jazzing up this cake by decorating the top with fresh strawberries? Place 4 medium strawberries in a colander or a strainer. Gently spray with lukewarm water. Shake to remove excess water. Stem the berries and then cut into quarters. Arrange a circle of strawberry quarters along the outside edge of the top of the cake.

Replace the strawberry preserves with your favorite red raspberry preserves, then make the finished cake truly pretty in pink by decorating the top with fresh red raspberries. If you feel compelled to continue your ardent ways, serve each slice in a pool of pureed raspberries, fresh or frozen.

This cake may be prepared over 2 days.

DAY 1: Bake the Schnappy Chocolate Cake layers. Once they're cooled, cover each layer with plastic wrap and refrigerate.

DAY 2: Make the Pretty in Pink Icing. Assemble the Pretty in Pink Cake. Refrigerate for 1 hour before serving.

After assembly, you may keep the Pretty in Pink Cake in the refrigerator for 2 to 3 days before serving. To avoid permeating the cake with refrigerator odors, place it in a large, tightly sealed plastic container.

Mrs. D's "She Ain't Heavy" Chocolate Cake

"SHE AIN'T HEAVY"
CHOCOLATE CAKE

1 tablespoon unsalted
butter, melted

3/4 pound (3 sticks) unsalted
butter, cut into 1/2-ounce
pieces

2 cups cake flour

3/4 cup unsweetened cocoa
powder

1 1/4 teaspoons baking soda

1/2 teaspoon baking powder

1/2 teaspoon salt

1 3/4 cups granulated sugar

3 large eggs

1 1/4 cups whole milk

1 teaspoon pure vanilla
extract

My mom (Mrs. D.) is an unabashed chocolate lover. Nothing chocolate escapes her appetite, be it an M&M's or, as in this recipe, the most perfect piece of chocolate cake you could possibly imagine passing your lips.

Yes, but if it's a heavy-duty chocolate cake, how come it doesn't contain any chocolate? For hundreds of years a beverage known as chocolate (early on this drink was served cold) was produced from the fruit of the cocoa tree (botanically known as *Theobroma cacao*). But why quibble, Mom knows best, and if she wants to call it chocolate, so be it. For the record, cocoa is derived by pressing out most of the cocoa butter from pure chocolate (known as chocolate liquor), yielding, well after further manipulation, both powdered unsweetened cocoa and baking chocolate.

MAKE MRS. D'S "SHE AIN'T HEAVY" CHOCOLATE CAKE
Preheat the oven to 350°F.

Lightly coat the insides of three 9 × 1 1/2-inch cake pans with some of the melted butter. Line the bottoms of the pans with parchment paper (or wax paper), then lightly coat the paper with more melted butter. Set aside.

In a sifter combine the cake flour, cocoa powder, baking soda, baking powder, and salt. Sift onto a large piece of parchment paper (or wax paper) and set aside.

Place the sugar and the 3/4 pound butter in the bowl of an electric mixer fitted with a paddle. Mix on low speed for 1 minute, then beat on medium until soft, about 2 minutes. Scrape down the sides of the bowl and the paddle. Continue beating on medium for an additional 2 minutes until very soft. Scrape down the sides of the bowl and the paddle. Add the eggs one at a time, beating on medium for 30 seconds after each addition, and scraping down the sides of the bowl once the eggs have been incorporated. Operate the mixer on low while gradually adding about half of the dry ingredients, followed by about half of the milk. Once these ingredients have been incorporated, about 1½ minutes, gradually add the remaining dry ingredients, followed by the remaining milk; mix until incorporated, about 1½ minutes. Scrape down the sides of the bowl and the paddle. Don't be concerned if the batter looks a bit odd texturally at this point (because of the interaction between the milk and butter); it will come together nicely with the next step.

Add the vanilla extract and mix on low for 5 seconds; beat on medium for 1 minute until thoroughly combined. Remove the bowl from the mixer and use a rubber spatula to finish mixing the ingredients until thoroughly combined. Now the batter looks very thick, a bit like soft-serve ice cream, but please don't taste, because the ingestion of raw yolks may not be salubrious. Immediately divide the cake batter among the prepared pans (about 2¼ cups in each pan), spreading evenly (an offset spatula would work best).

Bake on the top and center racks in the oven until a toothpick inserted in the center of each cake layer comes out clean, about 35 minutes. (Rotate the pans from top to center halfway through the baking time.) Remove the cake layers from the oven and cool in the pans for 15 to 20 minutes at room temperature. Invert the cake layers onto cake circles (or cake plates) wrapped with plastic wrap or lined with parchment paper or wax paper. Carefully peel the paper away from the bottoms of the layers. Refrigerate the cake layers while preparing the icing.

MAKE MRS. D'S "HASN'T FAILED ME YET" COCOA ICING

In a sifter combine the confectioners' sugar and cocoa powder. Sift onto an extra large (about 12 × 20 inches) piece of parchment paper (or wax paper) and set aside.

Place the butter in the bowl of an electric mixer fitted with a paddle. Mix on low speed for 1 minute; increase the speed to medium and beat for 2 minutes until soft. Use a rubber spatula to scrape down the sides of the bowl and the paddle. Beat on medium for 2 more minutes until very soft. Scrape down the sides of the bowl and paddle. Operate the mixer on the lowest speed (stir) while gradually adding about half the amount of dry ingredients, followed by half the amount of milk. Once these ingredients have been incorporated, about 2 minutes, add the remaining dry

"HASN'T FAILED ME YET"
COCOA ICING

1¼ pounds confectioners'
   sugar
1¼ cups unsweetened cocoa
   powder
1¼ pounds (5 sticks)
   unsalted butter, cut into
   ½-ounce pieces
½ cup whole milk
1 teaspoon pure vanilla
   extract

SERVES 12

ingredients, followed by the remaining milk; mix until incorporated, about 2 minutes. Scrape down the sides of the bowl and the paddle. Beat on medium for 1 more minute until very soft and fluffy. Add the vanilla extract and mix on low for 5 seconds; increase the speed to medium and beat for 1 minute until very soft and fluffy. Remove the bowl from the mixer and use a rubber spatula to finish mixing the icing until thoroughly combined.

ASSEMBLE MRS. D'S "SHE AIN'T HEAVY" CHOCOLATE CAKE
Remove the cake layers from the refrigerator. Turn one of the layers onto a clean cake circle (or cake plate), then peel off the paper. Use a cake spatula to spread 1½ cups of icing evenly and smoothly over the top and to the edges of the cake layer. Turn a second cake layer onto the iced layer, then peel off the paper. Use a cake spatula to spread 1½ cups of icing evenly and smoothly over the top and to the edges of the cake layer. Turn the remaining cake layer onto the second iced layer and gently press the layers into place. Spread the remaining icing over the top and sides of the entire cake. Refrigerate the cake for 1 hour before serving.

TO SERVE   Heat the blade of a serrated slicer under hot running water and wipe the blade dry before making each slice. Keep the slices at room temperature for 15 to 20 minutes before serving.

𝒯HE CHEF'S TOUCH

This cake may be prepared over 2 days.

DAY 1: Bake the "She Ain't Heavy" Chocolate Cake layers. Once they're cooled, cover each layer with plastic wrap and refrigerate.

DAY 2: Make the "Hasn't Failed Me Yet" Cocoa Icing. Assemble the cake as directed in the recipe. Refrigerate for 1 hour before serving.

After assembly, keep the cake in the refrigerator for 3 to 4 days before serving. To avoid permeating the cake with refrigerator odors, place it in a large, tightly sealed plastic container.

Chocolate "Just the Two of Us" Birthday Cake

Birthdays are a celebration of life, so what better ingredient to add to a jubilant birthday cake than natural honey? With over three hundred varieties of honey available, risk-taking bakers could be tempted to use bell heather, buckwheat, or even chestnut honey for this cake and icing. Avoid this temptation, since a zesty flavor could smother the sublime subtleties of this cake. That is why I suggest a mild-flavored clover honey to keep things from being too sweet, too pungent, or too overwhelming.

The perfect nectar for this birthday celebration would be an extremely cold and very dry sparkling wine.

MAKE THE CHOCOLATE HONEY SWIRL CAKE Preheat the oven to 350°F. Lightly coat the inside of a 6 × 3-inch aluminum cake pan using the melted butter. Flour the inside of the pan using the 2 teaspoons cake flour. Shake out any excess flour. Set aside.

In a sifter combine the ¾ cup cake flour and the baking powder. Sift onto a large piece of parchment paper (or wax paper) and set aside.

Place the 3 ounces butter in the bowl of an electric mixer fitted with a paddle. Mix on low speed for 1 minute, then beat on medium until soft, about 1 minute. Use a rubber spatula to scrape down the sides of the bowl and the paddle. Beat for 1 additional minute on medium until very soft. Scrape down the sides of the bowl and the paddle. Add the dry ingredients, heavy cream, and sugar and mix on the lowest speed (stir) to combine, about 30 seconds; mix on low for 30 additional seconds. Scrape down the sides of the bowl and the paddle. Add the egg yolks and honey and beat on medium for 1 minute. Scrape down the sides of the bowl and the paddle. Now beat on medium for an additional 30 seconds. Remove the bowl from the mixer and use a rubber spatula to finish mixing the ingredients until thoroughly combined. Transfer ½ cup of the

CHOCOLATE HONEY SWIRL CAKE

1 teaspoon unsalted butter, melted

3 ounces unsalted butter, cut into ¼-ounce pieces

¾ cup cake flour plus 2 teaspoons

½ teaspoon baking powder

¼ cup heavy cream

⅓ cup granulated sugar

2 large egg yolks

2 tablespoons clover honey

1 ounce semisweet baking chocolate, coarsely chopped and melted (see pages 20–21)

¼ cup warm water

¼ cup clover honey

4 tablespoons granulated
sugar

2 large egg whites

1 teaspoon unsweetened
cocoa powder

SERVES 2

honey batter into a small bowl with the semisweet chocolate and use a rubber spatula to stir until well combined.

Place about half (slightly more than ½ cup) of the remaining plain honey batter in the bottom of the prepared pan and smooth to the edges with a rubber spatula. Evenly spread the chocolate honey batter on top of the first layer of plain honey batter. Top the layer of chocolate batter with the remaining ½ cup or so of plain honey batter and spread evenly. Marbleize the cake by dipping the flat blade of a dinner knife all the way down into the batter, and then lifting the blade out in a folding motion like the roll of a wave, repeating about 6 times throughout the batter. Smooth the surface of the batter with a rubber spatula. Bake on the center rack in the oven until a toothpick inserted in the center of the cake comes out ever so slightly moist (almost but not quite dry), about 43 minutes. Remove the cake from the oven and cool in the pan at room temperature for 15 minutes. Invert the cake onto a cake circle (or onto a cake plate), then turn back over to top side up. Refrigerate on the circle or plate until cold, about 1 hour.

MAKE THE "HONEY, I'M ON CLOUD NINE" ICING   Measure the warm water into a Pyrex measuring cup, then add the honey. Transfer the water and honey to a small saucepan (the Pyrex cup makes this easier) and add 2 tablespoons of the sugar. Bring to a boil over medium-high heat. Boil the mixture, stirring occasionally, until it reaches a temperature of 240°F (for the candy makers this is the soft-ball stage), about 5 minutes. I recommend using a candy thermometer versus an instant-read thermometer for an accurate temperature reading. Remove the saucepan from the heat, then immediately place the egg whites and the remaining 2 tablespoons sugar in the bowl of an electric mixer fitted with a balloon whip. Whisk on high speed until soft peaks form, about 1 minute. Carefully and slowly add the honey mixture (it will be extremely hot) to the egg whites while whisking on high speed until the mixture is very thick, about 3 minutes. Remove the bowl from the mixer. Evenly spread the honey icing over the top and sides of the cake. Place the cocoa powder in a small sifter and sprinkle the cocoa over the cloud of icing. The cake can be cut immediately or refrigerated until you and your honey are ready to blow out the candles.

TO SERVE Heat the blade of a serrated slicer under hot running water and wipe the blade dry before making each slice. Serve immediately.

𝒯HE CHEF'S TOUCH

Be exotic and garnish the presentation plate with a chunk of pure, natural, comb honey. Available in a 4¼-inch square that is an inch thick and weighs about a pound, the comb slices like butter, and oh, my, how sweet it is!

The 6 × 3-inch aluminum cake pan used in this recipe is available from Wilton Enterprises online at www.wilton.com.

This cake may be prepared over 2 days.

*DAY 1: **Bake the Chocolate Honey Swirl Cake.*** Once it's cooled, cover with plastic wrap and refrigerate.

*DAY 2: **Make the "Honey, I'm on Cloud Nine" Icing.*** Assemble the Chocolate "Just the Two of Us" Birthday Cake. Serve immediately or refrigerate until needed.

After assembly, keep the cake in the refrigerator for 2 to 3 days before serving. To avoid permeating the cake with refrigerator odors, place it in a large, tightly sealed plastic container.

ROLF'S OLD-WORLD BLACK FOREST CAKE

VANILLA SUGAR COOKIE
BASE

1 teaspoon unsalted butter,
    melted

2 ounces (½ stick) unsalted
    butter, cut into ½-ounce
    pieces

1¼ cups all-purpose flour

¾ teaspoon baking
    powder

⅓ cup granulated sugar

1 large egg

1 tablespoon sour cream

1 teaspoon pure vanilla
    extract

¼ cup black currant
    preserves

OLD-WORLD COCOA
SPONGE CAKE

1 tablespoon unsalted
    butter, melted

3 ounces unsalted butter, cut
    into ½-ounce pieces

1½ cups all-purpose flour

½ cup unsweetened cocoa
    powder

8 large eggs

1 cup granulated sugar

When I decided to include a Black Forest cake in this book I turned for help to retired executive pastry chef Rolf Herion, who has been my good friend since 1970. When I first met Rolf, he was in charge of producing all the breads and desserts for the restaurants operated by the Colonial Williamsburg Foundation (including the prestigious Williamsburg Inn). Rolf was born in the town of Säckingen in the Black Forest region of Germany. During the years I worked at Colonial Williamsburg, I remember the countless letters written to Rolf complimenting him on his incomparable Black Forest cake. Rolf spent a day at Ganache Hill with Brett Bailey and me re-creating the famous cake that is a testament to the many years Rolf spent honing his craft. Rolf's version does not stint on ingredients. Layers of kirschwasser-soaked cocoa cake are interspersed with glazed fresh cherries and an elegant chocolate buttercream. The whole is lavishly spread with whipped cream and then topped with chocolate curls. This supreme dessert glorifies any celebration.

MAKE THE VANILLA SUGAR COOKIE BASE   Preheat the oven to 350°F.

Lightly coat the inside of a 9 × 1½-inch nonstick cake pan with the melted butter. Set aside.

In a sifter combine the flour and baking powder. Sift onto a large piece of parchment paper (or wax paper). Set aside.

Place the sugar and 2 ounces butter in the bowl of an electric mixer fitted with a paddle. Mix on low speed for 1 minute; then increase the speed to medium and beat for 2 minutes until soft. Use a rubber spatula to scrape down the sides of the bowl. Add the egg and beat on medium for 2 minutes until thoroughly combined. Scrape down the sides of the bowl and the paddle. Now beat on medium-high for 1 minute (although the mixture is not appealing in appearance, it will soon become an excellent cookie dough). Operate the mixer on low while gradually adding the dry ingredients; mix until incorporated, about 1 minute. Add the sour cream and vanilla extract and mix on medium until combined, about 15 seconds. Remove the bowl from the mixer and use a rubber spatula to finish mixing the ingredients until thoroughly combined (now you have something that looks like cookie dough). Transfer the dough to the prepared pan. Wearing a pair of disposable vinyl (or latex) gloves, evenly press the dough into the bottom of the pan from the center to the edges in a uniform thickness (this is easily done as the dough is very pliable).

Bake on the center rack in the oven until the edges of the cookie base are lightly golden brown and have started to pull away from the sides of the pan, 12 to 13 minutes. Remove the cookie base from the oven and cool in the pan at room temperature for 5 minutes. Invert onto a cake circle (or cake plate) and set aside to cool at room temperature for 20 minutes. Turn the cookie base over. Evenly spread the black currant preserves over the entire top surface of the cookie base. Refrigerate the cookie base.

MAKE THE OLD-WORLD COCOA SPONGE CAKE Preheat the oven to 350°F.

Lightly coat the insides of three 9 × 1½-inch nonstick cake pans with some of the melted butter. Line the bottoms of the pans with parchment paper (or wax paper), then lightly coat the paper with more melted butter. Set aside.

In a sifter combine the flour and cocoa powder. Sift onto a large piece of parchment paper (or wax paper) and set aside until needed. Place 3 ounces butter in a small glass bowl in a microwave oven set at medium power for 45 seconds. Remove and use a rubber spatula to stir the butter until melted, smooth, and creamy. (This microwave technique for melting yields a butter that has a sauce-like consistency and that is not warm—it must not be warm to the touch when added to the cake batter.)

Heat 1 inch of water in a large saucepan over medium heat. When the water begins to simmer, place the eggs and sugar in a large stainless steel bowl. Set the bowl into the saucepan (the bottom of the bowl should not touch the water). Using a handheld whisk (you may instead

¼ cup kirschwasser (clear cherry brandy)

GLAZED CHERRIES
1½ pounds fresh tart red cherries
¾ cup granulated sugar
2 tablespoons kirschwasser
3½ tablespoons water
2 tablespoons cornstarch

"JUST A HINT OF CHOCOLATE" BUTTERCREAM
½ pound (2 sticks) unsalted butter, cut into ½-ounce pieces
½ cup granulated sugar
4 large egg whites
4 ounces semisweet chocolate, coarsely chopped and melted (see pages 20–21)

WHIPPED CREAM
2¼ cups heavy cream
3 tablespoons granulated sugar

CHOCOLATE CURLS
2 ounces semisweet chocolate curls (see pages 19–20)

SERVES 12

use a handheld electric mixer fitted with the whisk attachment), gently whisk the eggs and sugar until the mixture reaches a temperature of 110°F, about 3½ minutes. Transfer the egg mixture to the bowl of an electric mixer fitted with a balloon whip. (Make certain that the bowl and whip are meticulously clean and dry; otherwise, the eggs will not whisk properly.) Whisk on high speed for 5 minutes until light and airy, and soft peaks have almost formed. (While being whisked, the mixture looks as though it may escape the mixing bowl; relax—it won't.) Remove the bowl from the mixer and use a rubber spatula to gently but thoroughly fold in about half the dry ingredients; once incorporated, fold in the remaining dry ingredients. Now fold the 3 ounces melted butter into the batter. Immediately divide the cake batter among the prepared pans (about 1¾ cups per pan) and spread it evenly.

Bake on the top and center racks in the oven until a toothpick inserted in the center of each cake layer comes out clean, 13 to 14 minutes. (Rotate the pans from the top to the center halfway through the baking time.) Remove the cake layers from the oven and cool in the pans for 10 minutes at room temperature. Invert the layers onto cake circles (or directly onto cake plates). Carefully peel the paper away from the bottoms of the layers. Use a pastry brush to moisten the top and sides equally of each of the layers with some of the kirschwasser. Wrap the layers with plastic wrap and refrigerate until ready to assemble.

GLAZE THE CHERRIES   Wash and dry the cherries. Reserve 12 of the prettiest cherries (with stems attached) to garnish the cake. Remove the stems and pits from the remaining cherries (you should end up with about 4 cups).

Heat the sugar, kirschwasser, and 2 tablespoons of the water in a small saucepan over medium heat. When hot, stir to dissolve the sugar. Bring to a boil. Add the cherries to the boiling liquid and stir to coat them (at this point it does not appear as though there is enough liquid to cook the cherries, but after a few minutes the cherries will give off enough liquid to get things going). Bring the mixture to a boil, then reduce the heat and cook the cherries at a simmer for 3 minutes until they are slightly soft. Whisk together the cornstarch and the remaining 1½ tablespoons of the water in a small bowl until the cornstarch is dissolved and the mixture is smooth. Add the cornstarch mixture to the simmering cherries and stir to thicken. Simmer for an additional 2 minutes. You will have 2½ cups. Transfer the cherries to a baking sheet with sides and refrigerate.

MAKE THE "JUST A HINT OF CHOCOLATE" BUTTERCREAM
Place the butter in the bowl of an electric mixer fitted with a paddle. Mix on low speed for 1 minute; increase the speed to medium and beat for 2 minutes to begin softening the butter. Scrape down the sides of the bowl and the paddle. Now beat on medium-high for 2 minutes until soft. Transfer the butter to a small bowl and set aside at room temperature.

Heat 1 inch of water in a large saucepan over medium heat. When the water begins to simmer, place the sugar and egg whites in a large stainless steel bowl. Set the bowl into the saucepan (the bottom of the bowl should not touch the water). Using a handheld whisk (you may instead use a handheld electric mixer fitted with the whisk attachment), gently whisk the sugar and egg whites until the mixture reaches a temperature of 140°F, about 3 minutes.

Transfer the heated egg white mixture to the bowl of an electric mixer fitted with a balloon whip. (Make certain that the bowl and whip are meticulously clean and dry; otherwise, the egg white mixture will not whisk properly.) Whisk on high for 5 minutes until fluffy and no longer warm to the touch. Add the semisweet chocolate and whisk on medium for 15 seconds until combined. Scrape down the sides of the bowl. Add the whipped butter and whisk on medium for 15 seconds to combine. Remove the bowl from the mixer and use a rubber spatula to finish mixing the ingredients until thoroughly combined. Transfer the buttercream to a pastry bag fitted with a medium straight tip.

BEGIN ASSEMBLING THE BLACK FOREST CAKE   Remove one of the cake layers from the refrigerator. Remove and discard the plastic wrap. Place the cake layer (kirschwasser-brushed side up) on top of the currant preserves–topped cookie base. Pipe a 1-inch-wide and ¾-inch-high ring of buttercream along the outside edge of the cake layer. Pipe a second ring of the buttercream, of the same proportions, about 1 inch away from the first ring. Pipe a 1-inch-wide and ¾-inch-high dollop of buttercream in the center of the cake layer. Refrigerate this cake and cookie layer.

Remove a second cake layer from the refrigerator and repeat the application of the buttercream as accomplished for the cake and cookie layer. Refrigerate until the buttercream has firmed, about 30 minutes.

Remove all the cake layers from the refrigerator. Generously fill the spaces between the buttercream on the cake and cookie base layer with the glazed cherries (this will use about 1¼ cups of the glazed cherries). Place the next cake layer, with the buttercream, on top of the cake and cookie layer. Fill the spaces between the buttercream with the remaining 1¼ cups glazed cherries. Place the remaining cake layer (kirschwasser-brushed side up) on the top of the second buttercream- and glazed-cherry layer, and press gently into place. Refrigerate the cake while preparing the whipped cream.

MAKE THE WHIPPED CREAM Place the heavy cream and sugar in the bowl of an electric mixer fitted with a balloon whip. Whisk on medium-high speed for 2 minutes until firm peaks form. You will have about 5 cups. Transfer 2 cups of the whipped cream to a pastry bag fitted with a large star tip.

FINISH THE CAKE ASSEMBLY Spread the remaining 3 cups whipped cream over the top and sides of the cake. Pipe a circle of stars (each touching the other) along the outside edge of the top of the cake. Continue to pipe out circles of stars until the top of the cake is covered. Space the 12 reserved cherries evenly along the outside edge of the top of the cake. Decorate the top of the cake with chocolate curls. Refrigerate for 3 to 4 hours before serving.

TO SERVE Heat the blade of a serrated slicer under hot running water and wipe the blade dry before cutting each slice. Keep the slices at room temperature for about 15 minutes before serving.

The CHEF'S TOUCH

Kirschwasser is a limpid fruit brandy made from black cherries; it has its origins in the Black Forest region of Germany. Although other countries produce kirsch, the best is still made in the Black Forest. If you are unable to locate kirsch, substitute framboise, which is made from raspberries, or any other colorless fruit brandy that you find appealing.

You will find an astonishing array of preserves, jams, and fruit spreads at most upscale supermarket and gourmet specialty stores. If your taste preferences doesn't run to black currant preserves, please feel free to substitute a favorite. For me that would be red raspberry preserves.

This cake may be prepared over 2 days.

DAY 1: Bake the Vanilla Sugar Cookie Base. Once it's cooled, cover with plastic wrap and refrigerate overnight. Also bake the Old-World Cocoa Sponge Cake layers. After the cake layers have been out of the oven for 10 minutes, invert them and then brush with kirschwasser as described in the recipe. Once they're cooled to room temperature, cover with plastic wrap, and refrigerate overnight. Glaze the cherries. Once they're cooled, refrigerate.

DAY 2: Prepare the "Just a Hint of Chocolate" Buttercream. Remove the Vanilla Sugar Cookie Base from the refrigerator. Spread the black currant preserves over the cookie. Begin assembling the cake as described in the recipe. Make the whipped cream. Finish assembling the cake. Refrigerate the cake in a large, tightly sealed plastic container for 3 to 4 hours before serving.

After assembly, keep the cake in the refrigerator for 2 days before serving. To avoid permeating the cake with refrigerator odors, place it in a large, tightly sealed plastic container.

April Birthday Girl's Angelic Cocoa Roll

1 ounce melted unsalted
   butter plus 2 teaspoons
1/3 cup all-purpose flour
3 tablespoons unsweetened
   cocoa powder
1/2 teaspoon baking powder
1/4 teaspoon salt
1/2 cup granulated sugar
3 large eggs, separated
1 tablespoon red raspberry
   liqueur
1/2 cup red raspberry
   preserves

RED RASPBERRY—ALMOND
FILLING

2 cups heavy cream
1/3 cup confectioners' sugar,
   sifted
1 cup sliced almonds,
   toasted (see page 23) and
   lightly crushed by hand
1/2 cup red raspberry
   preserves
1 teaspoon pure vanilla
   extract

Tradition! That's what birthdays are all about. Although this heavenly cake breaks with tradition in its shape, the delicate texture of the cocoa layer spread generously with a light filling of almond and raspberry-enhanced whipped cream is bound to assuage even the most stodgy birthday girl or guy.

MAKE THE COCOA SPONGE CAKE   Preheat the oven to 375°F.

Lightly coat a 17¼ × 11½ × 1-inch jelly roll pan with some of the 2 teaspoons melted butter. Line the bottom of the pan with parchment paper (or wax paper), then lightly coat the paper with more melted butter. Set aside.

In a sifter combine the flour, cocoa powder, baking powder, and salt. Sift onto a large piece of parchment paper (or wax paper) and set aside until needed.

Place ¼ cup of the granulated sugar, the egg yolks, and the raspberry liqueur in the bowl of an electric mixer fitted with a paddle. Beat on medium-high speed for 4 minutes until the mixture is pale in color and slightly thickened, and the sugar is almost completely dissolved. (Rub a small amount of batter between your thumb and index finger; the batter should feel pretty smooth with very little grittiness. Don't lick your fingers, however—though the batter may look appealing, it contains raw egg yolks.) Operate the mixer on low while gradually adding the dry ingredients; mix until incorporated, about 45 seconds. Scrape down the sides of the bowl. Add the 1 ounce melted butter and mix on medium speed for 15 seconds to combine. The mixture will be thick. Transfer the mixture to a large bowl and set aside while whisking the egg whites.

Place the remaining ¼ cup granulated sugar and the egg whites in the bowl of an electric mixer fitted with a balloon whip. (Make certain that the bowl and whip are meticulously clean and dry; otherwise, the egg white mixture will not whisk properly). Whisk the egg whites and sugar on high speed for 3 minutes until stiff peaks form. Remove the bowl from the mixer. Transfer the egg whites to the large bowl with the cocoa–egg yolk mixture and use a rubber spatula to quickly fold in the whites until the mixture has a uniform milk chocolate color. Transfer the batter to the prepared jelly roll pan, spreading it evenly to the edges (an offset spatula will work best). Don't worry that the layer of batter is quite thin. The eggs will leaven the batter and supply the right amount of volume.

Place the pan on the center rack of the oven and bake for 9 to 10 minutes, until a toothpick inserted into the center of the cake comes out clean, and the edges start to pull away from the sides of the pan. Remove the cake from the oven and cool in the pan at room temperature for 10 minutes. Invert the cake onto a 12 × 20-inch piece of parchment paper (or wax paper). If any of the edges of the cake have not pulled away from the sides of the pan, use a sharp, thin-bladed paring knife to carefully cut the cake away from the sides. Gently peel the paper away from the bottom of the cake and discard. Place another 12 × 20-inch piece of paper over the cake (the side facing up now), and invert the cake again. Remove the top piece of paper and discard. Spread the red raspberry preserves, in a thin layer, to the edges of the cake. Set the cake aside at room temperature.

MAKE THE RED RASPBERRY–ALMOND FILLING Place the heavy cream and confectioners' sugar in the bowl of an electric mixer fitted with a balloon whip. Whisk on medium-high speed for 1½ minutes until firm but not stiff peaks form. Add the almonds, raspberry preserves, and vanilla extract and whisk on medium speed for 10 seconds. Remove the bowl from the mixer and use a rubber spatula to finish mixing until thoroughly combined. Refrigerate for 15 minutes.

ASSEMBLE THE COCOA ROLL Using a spatula (an offset spatula would be best), spread the raspberry-almond filling over the raspberry preserve–coated side of the cake, spreading evenly to the edges. Starting with the narrow side (the 10-inch width side) nearest you, roll the cake away from you, using the paper to help lift the cake over onto itself. Continue to roll the cake to the opposite end, making a tight roll. Now wrap the paper around the rolled cake (which is now a cocoa roll). Use a utility

ANGELIC GARNISH

3 tablespoons confectioners' sugar

2 to 3 teaspoons unsweetened cocoa powder

SERVES 8 TO 10

turner (wide spatula) to place the cocoa roll on a baking sheet. Refrigerate for 1 hour before garnishing.

GARNISH THE COCOA ROLL Remove the cocoa roll from the refrigerator. Unwrap the roll and discard the paper. Use a sharp knife or a serrated slicer to cut away about ½ inch from each end of the roll (consider the ends a treat for the cook). Place the roll back on a baking sheet. Dust as much of the top and sides of the cake as possible with the confectioners' sugar. Place a decorating stencil of your choice (see The Chef's Touch, below) on top of the cake and dust the cut-out areas of the stencil with 2 to 3 teaspoons cocoa powder, depending on the stencil. Remove the stencil, then refrigerate the roll for 1 hour before serving.

TO SERVE Use a sharp knife or a serrated slicer to cut the roll into the desired number of slices. Heat the blade of the knife or slicer under hot running water and wipe the blade dry before making each cut. The April birthday girl recommends serving each slice with a handful of fresh red raspberries and a surfeit of whipped cream. "Smashing!"

THE CHEF'S TOUCH

Our April birthday girl is Janeen Sarlin, the owner and executive chef of Cooking With Class, Inc., a catering company and cooking school in New York City. Janeen is also a cookbook writer. The dedication in her book *50 Ways to Feed Your Lover* tells a lot about the girl: "With love from Janeen to the men in my life who have tasted with the same fork and sipped from the same glass." Her cocoa roll recipe is a family favorite that was perfected many years ago by her Grams Broadwater. Janeen describes her cake as "smashing, delicious, light, and slightly sinful." I think you will agree.

This cake is very versatile. Many other preserves could be used and, for that matter, if the season is bursting with fresh berries—go for it.

A jelly roll pan, not a baking sheet, is necessary for this recipe. A regular baking sheet with ½-inch deep sides is too shallow, whereas a jelly roll pan is from ¾ to 1 inch deep.

Decorating stencils that celebrate birthdays and every other imaginable event can be readily fashioned by the clever, or purchased from kitchenware stores or online (see Online Sources, page 161).

CHOCOLATE MADRAS CAKE

Cranberries are one of only three fruits native to North America (Concord grapes and my beloved blueberry are the other two). Fresh, crimson cranberries are so tart on their own they can turn a palate inside out. However, just a bit of sugar tames fresh cranberries but leaves that audacious punch that people love. The unconventional alliance of fresh cranberries, orange, and chocolate hints of a conspiracy, yet this delightful confection is based on a popular cocktail, the Madras.

MAKE THE CRANBERRY COMPOTE Place the contents of the bag of cranberries in a colander and spray with lukewarm water. Shake the colander to remove excess water. Heat the cranberries, granulated sugar, vodka, orange juice, and orange zest in a medium saucepan over medium heat. When the mixture begins to simmer, adjust the heat and continue to simmer (not boil) for 10 to 11 minutes until the mixture is syrupy and most of the cranberries have popped open. Remove from the heat and transfer to large dinner plate, then refrigerate uncovered.

MAKE THE CHOCOLATE ORANGE MOUSSE CAKE Preheat the oven to 325°F. Lightly coat the insides of three 9 × 1½-inch nonstick cake pans with some of the melted butter. Line the bottoms of the pans with parchment paper (or wax paper), then lightly coat the paper with more melted butter. Set aside.

Melt the ½ pound butter and the semisweet chocolate in the top half of a double boiler, or in a medium glass bowl in a microwave oven, and stir until smooth.

Place the egg yolks, 1 cup of the granulated sugar, the orange zest, and orange extract in the bowl of an electric mixer fitted with a paddle. Beat on medium-high speed until thickened and pale yellow in color, about 4 minutes. Use a rubber spatula to scrape down the sides of the bowl, then beat on medium-high for 2 minutes until the sugar is almost completely dissolved. (You may savor the pleasant creamsicle aroma of

CRANBERRY COMPOTE

One 12-ounce bag (about 3½ cups) fresh (or frozen) whole cranberries

½ cup granulated sugar

¼ cup cranberry-flavored vodka

2 tablespoons fresh orange juice

1 teaspoon minced orange zest

CHOCOLATE ORANGE MOUSSE CAKE

1 tablespoon unsalted butter, melted

½ pound (2 sticks) unsalted butter, cut into ½-ounce pieces

6 ounces semisweet baking chocolate, coarsely chopped and melted (see pages 20–21)

9 large egg yolks

1 cup granulated sugar plus 2 tablespoons

1 tablespoon minced orange zest

1 teaspoon pure orange extract

4 large egg whites

12 ounces semisweet baking
   chocolate, coarsely
   chopped

4 ounces unsweetened
   baking chocolate, coarsely
   chopped

2 cups heavy cream

2 tablespoons granulated
   sugar

1 cup walnuts, toasted
   (see page 23) and coarsely
   chopped by hand with a
   cook's knife

THE FINAL TOUCH

1 cup walnuts, toasted
   (see page 23) and coarsely
   chopped by hand with a
   cook's knife

1 teaspoon minced orange
   zest

SERVES 10

the batter, but please keep your appetite at bay; consuming raw egg yolks may be harmful to your health.) Add the butter and chocolate mixture and beat on medium for 15 seconds. Scrape down the sides of the bowl. Beat on medium for an additional 10 seconds until thoroughly combined. Transfer the batter to a large bowl and set aside while whisking the egg whites.

Place the egg whites and the remaining 2 tablespoons granulated sugar in the bowl of an electric mixer fitted with a balloon whip. (Make certain that the bowl and whip are meticulously clean and dry; otherwise, the egg white mixture will not whisk properly). Whisk the egg whites and sugar on high speed for 1¼ minutes, until stiff peaks form. Remove the bowl from the mixer. Transfer half the egg whites to the bowl with the chocolate–egg yolk mixture and use a rubber spatula to quickly fold the mixture together, then gently fold in the remaining whites until the mixture has a uniform chocolate color.

Immediately divide the cake batter among the prepared pans (about 2 cups of batter in each pan) and spread it evenly (a small offset spatula works best). Bake on the top and center racks in the oven until a toothpick inserted in the center of each cake layer comes out not quite clean (just a crumb or so of batter will adhere to the toothpick), about 24 minutes. (Rotate the pans from top to center halfway through the baking time.) Remove the cake layers from the oven and cool in the pans for 15 minutes at room temperature. Using a thin-bladed paring knife, cut around the inside edges of the pan to release the cake layers. Invert the cake layers onto cake circles (or cake plates). If necessary, peel the paper away from the bottom of the cake layers. (I say "if necessary" because the paper usually sticks to the pan with this particular cake.) Refrigerate the cake layers.

PREPARE THE QUINTESSENTIAL CHOCOLATE GANACHE Place the chopped semisweet chocolate and unsweetened chocolate in a large bowl.

Heat the heavy cream and sugar in a small saucepan over medium-high heat. When hot, stir to dissolve the sugar. Bring to a boil. Pour the boiling cream over the chocolate, then stir with a whisk until smooth. Transfer 1 cup of the ganache to a baking sheet with sides (this ganache will be used to pipe stars onto the top of the cake) and spread evenly.

Refrigerate. In a medium bowl combine 1 cup of the ganache, 1 cup of the cranberry compote and the walnuts. Set the remaining ganache aside at room temperature.

ASSEMBLE THE CAKE Remove the cake layers from the refrigerator. Use a cake spatula to spread half the amount of the cranberry-walnut-ganache mixture over the top and out to the edges of one of the cake layers. Top with a second cake layer. Spread the remaining cranberry-walnut-ganache mixture over this layer; top with the last cake layer. Place the cake in the freezer for 30 minutes.

Remove the cake from the freezer. Transfer the room-temperature ganache to the top of the cake. Use a cake spatula to spread the ganache over the top and sides of the cake. Refrigerate the cake for 30 minutes.

Transfer the chilled ganache to a pastry bag fitted with a small star tip. Pipe a circle of chocolate stars (each one touching the next) along the outside edge of the top of the cake. (If the ganache in the pastry bag is too firm to pipe, keep it at room temperature until it is pliable. Keep the cake refrigerated until the ganache is pliable enough to pipe.) As a final touch, press the walnuts into the sides of the cake, coating them evenly. Spoon the remaining cranberry compote onto the top of the cake and spread to the edges of the chocolate stars. Sprinkle 1 teaspoon of minced orange zest over the cranberry compote. Refrigerate the cake for 2 hours before serving.

TO SERVE Heat the blade of a serrated slicer under hot running water and wipe the blade dry before cutting each slice. Place slices on serving plates and keep at room temperature for 10 to 15 minutes before serving.

*T*HE CHEF'S TOUCH

Use a sharp vegetable peeler to remove the orange zest (the colored skin of the orange). Don't use the bitter white pith under the skin. Once the colored skin has been removed, use a very sharp cook's knife to cut the skin into julienne as thin as possible, then mince the julienne.

This cake may be prepared over 2 days.

DAY 1: Make the Cranberry Compote. Refrigerate on a plate until cold, then cover with plastic wrap and keep in the refrigerator until needed (the compote will keep for several days in the refrigerator). Bake the Chocolate Orange Mousse Cake layers. Once the layers have cooled, cover with plastic wrap and refrigerate.

DAY 2: Prepare the Quintessential Chocolate Ganache with Walnuts as directed in the recipe, then assemble the cake. Refrigerate the cake for 2 hours. Slice and serve as directed in the recipe.

You may keep the cake in the refrigerator for 2 to 3 days before serving. To avoid permeating the cake with refrigerator odors, place it in a large, tightly sealed plastic container.

To double your pleasure, with this cake serve the Madras cocktail that inspired it.

2 ounces vodka
2 ounces cranberry juice
2 ounces fresh orange juice

Pour vodka and juices into a large old-fashioned glass filled with ice. Stir well.

Dancing Gingerbread Men Peppermint Fudge Cake

For many years, my wife, Connie, and I played Santa's helpers on Christmas Eve by delivering special holiday desserts to a number of our friends. The list was rather modest when we started the tradition some fifteen years ago, but as such things go, the list grew. Although it was fun driving all over town making the rounds, we tended to get a bit too merry with so many people offering us the requisite Christmas cheer. In December 1998, we decided it would be safer to invite our friends to Ganache Hill, where we would offer a glass of cheer, a cup of hot soup, and our customary holiday treat. The party was held on December 23 to give us Christmas Eve "off." The Dancing Gingerbread Men Peppermint Fudge Cake, designed by pastry chef Kelly Bailey, received greater reviews than we could have imagined. Picture a circle of gingerbread men dancing on layers of spicy, chocolaty fudge cake, bridged by two different white chocolate mousses, both redolent of candy, peppermint, and chocolate mini-morsels, then all lavishly covered with dark chocolate ganache. Beginning that night and into Christmas Eve, Williamsburg suffered under a record-breaking ice storm that left most of the city without power for up to six days. Our cake evidently brightened a lot of darkened homes. Including ours.

MAKE THE SPICY FUDGE CAKE Preheat the oven to 325°F. Lightly coat the insides of three 9 × 1½-inch nonstick cake pans with some of the melted butter. Line the bottoms of the pans with parchment paper (or wax paper), then lightly coat the paper with more melted butter. Set aside.

In a sifter combine the cake flour, ginger, cinnamon, baking soda, and salt. Sift onto a large piece of parchment paper (or wax paper) and set aside.

Place the light brown sugar and the 3 ounces of butter in the bowl of

SPICY FUDGE CAKE

1 tablespoon unsalted
   butter, melted

3 ounces unsalted butter, cut
   into ½-ounce pieces

1¾ cups cake flour

1 tablespoon ground
   ginger

1 teaspoon ground
   cinnamon

½ teaspoon baking soda

¼ teaspoon salt

¾ cup (6 ounces) tightly
   packed light brown sugar

3 large eggs

2 ounces unsweetened
   baking chocolate, coarsely
   chopped and melted
   (see pages 20–21)

¾ cup sour cream

½ cup hot water

¼ cup cinnamon schnapps

WHITE CHOCOLATE MOUSSE

2 cups heavy cream

6 ounces white chocolate,
   coarsely chopped and
   melted (see pages 20–21)

4 ounces unwrapped
   peppermint candy (22 or
   so 1-inch-diameter
   candies), chopped by
   hand into 1/8-inch
   pieces
1/2 cup semisweet chocolate
   mini-morsels

DANCING GINGERBREAD
MEN
1/2 cup all-purpose flour plus
   2 tablespoons
1/2 teaspoon ground allspice
1/2 teaspoon ground
   cinnamon
1/2 teaspoon ground ginger
1/8 teaspoon baking soda
1/8 teaspoon ground cloves
1 ounce unsalted butter
2 tablespoons (1 ounce)
   tightly packed dark
   brown sugar
1 large egg yolk
1 tablespoon "mild flavor"
   molasses (such as
   Grandma's brand
   unsulfured)

QUINTESSENTIAL
CHOCOLATE GANACHE
12 ounces semisweet baking
   chocolate, coarsely
   chopped
4 ounces unsweetened
   baking chocolate,
   coarsely chopped

an electric mixer fitted with a paddle. Mix on low speed for 1 minute, then beat on medium-high for 3 minutes until soft. Use a rubber spatula to scrape down the sides of the bowl, then beat on medium-high for an additional 3 minutes until very soft. Scrape down the sides of the bowl. Add the eggs, one at a time, beating on medium for 30 seconds after each addition; scrape down the sides of the bowl and the paddle once all the eggs have been incorporated (at this juncture the batter appears to be separating, but it will come together in the next step when the chocolate is added). Add the unsweetened chocolate and mix on medium for 10 seconds. Operate the mixer on low while gradually adding the dry ingredients; mix until incorporated, about 1 minute. Add the sour cream and mix on medium to combine, about 30 seconds. Add the hot water in a slow, steady stream and mix on the lowest speed to combine, about 30 seconds. Add the cinnamon schnapps and mix on low to combine, about 15 seconds. Remove the bowl from the mixer and use a rubber spatula to finish mixing the ingredients until thoroughly combined. Immediately divide the cake batter among the prepared pans (about 1 1/2 cups of batter in each pan) and spread evenly (not much spreading is necessary, as the batter is not very thick).

Bake on the top and center racks in the oven until a toothpick inserted in the center of the cake layers comes out clean, about 22 minutes (rotate the pans from top to center halfway through the baking time). Remove the cake layers from the oven and cool in the pans for 15 minutes at room temperature. Invert the cake layers onto cake circles (or cake plates). Carefully peel the paper away from the bottoms of the layers. Refrigerate the layers.

MAKE THE WHITE CHOCOLATE MOUSSE   Place the heavy cream in the bowl of an electric mixer fitted with a balloon whip. Whisk on medium-high for 1 1/2 minutes until firm but not stiff peaks form. Add about 1 cup of the whipped cream to the white chocolate (make certain that the bowl containing the white chocolate has no residual heat from the melting of the chocolate; otherwise, the ingredients will lose a lot of volume when combined; if the bowl is warm, transfer the white chocolate to a room-temperature bowl), and use a rubber spatula to fold them together until thoroughly combined. Add the whipped cream and white chocolate mixture to the remaining whipped cream and use a rubber spatula to fold them together until smooth and thoroughly combined. Divide the white chocolate mousse into 2 medium bowls (about 2 cups of mousse in each bowl). Add the peppermint candy to one bowl and the chocolate mini-morsels to the other bowl. Use a rubber spatula to fold together the ingredients in each bowl until thoroughly combined. Refrigerate the 2 bowls of mousse for 15 minutes, then begin assembling the cake.

BEGIN THE CAKE ASSEMBLY   Remove the cake layers from the refrigerator. Use a cake spatula to evenly and smoothly spread the peppermint candy–enhanced White Chocolate Mousse over the top and to the edges of one of the cake layers, and set aside for a few moments. Use a cake spatula to evenly and smoothly spread the chocolate mini-morsel–laden White Chocolate Mousse over the top and to the edges of a second cake layer, then top this layer with the last cake layer. Use a utility turner (wide spatula) to transfer the two layers onto the layer with the peppermint mousse and gently press the layers into place. Refrigerate the cake for 2 to 3 hours, until the mousse layers are firm, before making the ganache.

MAKE THE DANCING GINGERBREAD MEN   While the mousse layered cake is in the refrigerator, make the Dancing Gingerbread Men.

Preheat the oven to 325°F.

In a sifter combine the ½ cup flour, the allspice, cinnamon, ginger, baking soda, and cloves. Sift onto a large piece of parchment paper (or wax paper) and set aside.

Place the butter, brown sugar, egg yolk, and molasses in the bowl of a food processor fitted with a metal blade. Process for 15 seconds. Add the dry ingredients and pulse for 10 seconds, then process for 45 seconds. Scrape down the sides of the bowl, then remove the dough and form it into a smooth ball.

Place the dough ball onto a clean, dry, lightly floured work surface. Roll the dough (using the 2 tablespoons flour as necessary to prevent sticking) into a square about 7 × 7 inches and ¼ inch thick. Cut the dough into about 26 gingerbread men, using a small gingerbread man cutter (1½ inches tall and 1 inch wide). Form the remaining dough into a ball; roll into a square about 4 × 4 inches and ¼ inch thick. Cut the dough into about 12 gingerbread men, using the gingerbread man cutter

2 cups heavy cream

2 tablespoons granulated
   sugar

SERVES 12

(there may be some extra dough; if so, roll and cut even more ginger-bread men). Place the gingerbread men, evenly spaced, onto a nonstick baking sheet. Bake on the center rack of the oven for 11 to 12 minutes (turn the sheet 180 degrees about halfway through the baking time). Remove the gingerbread men from the oven and cool on the baking sheets at room temperature until ready to finish assembling the cake.

PREPARE THE QUINTESSENTIAL CHOCOLATE GANACHE Place the chopped semisweet chocolate and unsweetened chocolate in a large bowl.

Heat the heavy cream and sugar in a small saucepan over medium-high heat. When hot, stir to dissolve the sugar. Bring to a boil. Pour the boiling cream over the chocolate, then stir with a whisk until smooth. Transfer 1 cup of the ganache to a baking sheet with sides (this ganache will be used to pipe stars onto the top of the cake) and spread evenly. Refrigerate. Set the remaining ganache aside for a few minutes.

FINISH ASSEMBLING THE CAKE Remove the cake from the refrigerator. Smooth the mousse on the sides of the cake with a cake spatula. Place a cooling rack on a baking sheet with sides. Use a utility turner (wide spatula) to transfer the whole cake from the cake circle onto the cooling rack. Ladle two 4-ounce ladles of the ganache over the top of the cake. Use a cake spatula to spread a smooth coating of ganache over the top and sides of the cake. Refrigerate the cake for 15 to 20 minutes to set the ganache. Remove the cake from the refrigerator and pour the remaining ganache over the top of the cake, allowing the ganache to flow down the sides of the cake, completely enrobing it with a smooth coating of ganache (if the ganache is not flowing as described, assist it with a cake spatula).

Use the utility turner to transfer the cake onto a clean cardboard cake circle. Refrigerate the cake for 15 to 20 minutes to set the ganache. Any remaining ganache may be formed into truffles (see page 143), or decadently dispatched with fingers or spoon.

Fill a pastry bag fitted with a medium star tip with the reserved 1 cup of ganache. Pipe a circle of 24 chocolate ganache stars (each touching the other) along the outside edge of the top of the cake. Refrigerate for 1 hour before slicing and serving.

TO SERVE Heat the blade of a serrated slicer under hot running water and wipe the blade dry before cutting each slice. Place cake slices cut side down on each serving plate (rather than standing). The gingerbread men may be used to decorate the sides and top of the cake slices or placed as a garnish directly on the individual serving plates (that is, as long as the baker and helpers have not already eaten them). You may also want to decorate each slice with a piece of peppermint candy (do so just before serving; otherwise, the candy will dissolve if it is placed on the cake and then refrigerated). Serve immediately.

𝒯HE CHEF'S TOUCH

Ground ginger is sometimes labeled powdered ginger. No matter the label, it should be purchased in small containers, since it loses its charm when exposed to air. I usually caution a sparing hand when using ground ginger because of its assertive flavor. This spice cake, however, is spiked with a generous tablespoon of ground ginger, which gives it a lively yet not overwhelming spiciness.

We used Fire Water Hot Cinnamon Schnapps when we tested the Spicy Fudge Cake. Produced in Lewiston, Maine, this schnapps has a flavor that stands up to other ingredients and doesn't fade during baking.

You can find 1-pound bags of peppermint candies at the supermarket (they're fat free, the bag says!), or look for the individually wrapped peppermints in the bulk food section.

I usually recommended Plantation brand blackstrap molasses for both savory and sweet recipes, but it blew the spices of this gingerbread cookie out of the ballpark. A more subtly flavored molasses, such as Grandma's brand unsulfured was more compatible.

Holiday oriented baking paraphernalia usually appears at your local supermarket a couple of weeks or so before Thanksgiving. That's where and when we found our small (1½ inch high and 1 inch wide) gingerbread man cutter.

Consider doubling or even quadrupling the Dancing Gingerbread Men recipe—we did! Once baked and cooled, the gingerbread men can be stored at room temperature in a tightly sealed plastic container for up to a week. For long-term storage, up to several weeks, freeze the gingerbread men in a tightly sealed plastic container to prevent dehydration and to protect them from freezer odor.

This cake may be prepared over 3 days.

DAY 1: Bake the Spicy Fudge Cake layers. Once they're cooled, cover each layer with plastic wrap and refrigerate overnight. Also bake the Dancing Gingerbread Men. Once they're cooled to room temperature, store in a covered container at room temperature.

DAY 2: Make the White Chocolate Mousse. Divide the mousse in half and add peppermint candy and chocolate mini-morsels as described in the recipe. Spread the cake layers with mousse; assemble the layers. Refrigerate the cake in a large, tightly sealed plastic container.

DAY 3: Prepare the Quintessential Chocolate Ganache. Cover the cake with ganache. Decorate with ganache stars. Refrigerate for 1 hour. Slice and garnish as directed in the recipe. Serve.

After assembly, you may keep the cake in the refrigerator for 2 days before serving. To avoid permeating the cake with refrigerator odors, place it in a large, tightly sealed plastic container.

BOB'S BIG-ASS CHOCOLATE BROWN SUGAR AND BOURBON BIRTHDAY CAKE

'Scuse me, but it's the cake that's big. Danger lurks when a group of Leos gathers for a communal birthday celebration. "Leos of Williamsburg unite" was the rallying cry from my spirited friend and fellow Leo, Bob Hawkins, a few years ago. And unite we did, as a dozen Leos and their friends threw a raucous birthday party at a local den. Being of generous nature, the lions brought much food and drink. My offering was a mountainous cake fashioned by Trellis pastry chef Kelly Bailey. Upon unveiling the cake, Bob Hawkins uttered, "man, that's a big-ass cake." This humongous cake will feed a gang of any size. One big wedge of chocolate cake, 8 layers deep, 7 inches wide, and 10 inches high, gets its kick from bourbon as well as from the oversize visual pun. Grab the pitchfork and have a bite.

MAKE THE CHOCOLATE BROWN SUGAR AND BOURBON CAKE
Preheat the oven to 325°F.

Lightly coat two 15¼ × 10¼ × ¾-inch nonstick baking sheets (do not substitute a different size baking sheet) with some of the melted butter. Line the bottoms of the sheets with parchment paper (or wax paper), then lightly coat the paper with more melted butter. Set aside.

In a sifter combine the flour, cocoa powder, baking powder, baking soda, and salt. Sift onto a large piece of parchment paper (or wax paper) and set aside.

Place the brown sugar and eggs in the bowl of an electric mixer fitted with a paddle. Beat on medium-high speed for 3 minutes until the mixture is thoroughly combined and has thickened. Add the semisweet chocolate and beat on medium until incorporated, about 30 seconds. Use a rubber spatula to scrape down the sides of the bowl. Operate the

CHOCOLATE BROWN SUGAR
AND BOURBON CAKE

1 tablespoon unsalted butter, melted

1¾ cups all-purpose flour

½ cup unsweetened cocoa powder

½ teaspoon baking powder

½ teaspoon baking soda

¼ teaspoon salt

1 cup (8 ounces) tightly packed light brown sugar

2 large eggs

4 ounces semisweet baking chocolate, coarsely chopped and melted (see pages 20–21)

½ cup vegetable oil

⅓ cup 100% pure U.S. Grade A dark amber maple syrup

⅓ cup bourbon whiskey

½ cup sour cream

CHOCOLATE BOURBON BUTTERCREAM

10 ounces semisweet baking
    chocolate, coarsely
    chopped
1 cup heavy cream
½ cup granulated sugar
¼ cup bourbon whiskey
¾ pound (3 sticks) unsalted
    butter, cut into ½-ounce
    pieces

SERVES 12 TO 16

mixer on medium while slowly adding the vegetable oil in a steady stream (to prevent splattering oil outside of the bowl, use a pouring shield attachment or cover the top of the mixer down the sides to the bowl with a towel or plastic wrap), about 1 minute. Gradually add the maple syrup and mix on medium until incorporated, about 30 seconds. Scrape down the sides of the bowl. Operate the mixer on the lowest speed (stir) while gradually adding half the dry ingredients; mix until incorporated, about 45 seconds. Add the bourbon whiskey and mix on low to incorporate, about 30 seconds. Once again operate the mixer on the lowest speed and gradually add the remaining dry ingredients; mix until incorporated, about 30 seconds. Scrape down the sides of the bowl and the paddle. Add the sour cream and mix on medium until incorporated, about 15 seconds. Remove the bowl from the mixer and use a rubber spatula to finish mixing the batter until thoroughly combined (the aroma of the batter and its fudge-like appearance will certainly stimulate your chocolate appetite; suppress that desire to consume raw eggs and wait until after the cake is baked to steal a taste).

Immediately divide the batter into the prepared baking sheets (about 2⅛ cups of batter for each sheet) and spread as evenly as possible (to ensure baked layers with a uniformly flat surface) to the inside edges of the baking sheet with an offset spatula. Bake on the top and center racks in the oven until a toothpick inserted into the center of each cake layer comes out ever so slightly moist and the edges of the cakes start to pull away from the sides of the sheets, 13 to 14 minutes (rotate the sheets from top to center and turn 180 degrees halfway through the baking time). Remove the cake layers from the oven and set aside for 4 to 5 minutes at room temperature, until the sheets can be handled with bare hands (the cakes will be easier to remove from the sheets at this point than when they are completely cool). Invert each layer onto an 18 × 12-inch piece of parchment paper (or wax paper) by firmly tapping one side of the edge of the baking sheet against the paper on the work surface. Peel the paper away from the bottom of each cake.

Place one of the cake layers on a clean, dry cutting board (leaving it on the paper). Use a sharp serrated slicer to trim ½ inch of cake from each of the short ends. These trimmings were made for eating, so you may now steal a bite of perfectly baked cake. Use the slicer to cut a small mark, directly in the center, on the edge of the long end of the cake side closest to you. Rotate the cake 180 degrees. Now mark this long edge 3½ inches away from each short end (there should be two marks). Cut the cake into 3 equal size triangular pieces and 2 half triangles. Set aside, then repeat with the second cake layer. Place the pieces of both cake layers, uncovered, in the refrigerator while preparing the buttercream.

PREPARE THE CHOCOLATE BOURBON BUTTERCREAM Place the chopped semisweet chocolate in a large bowl. Heat the heavy cream and sugar in a small saucepan over medium heat. When hot, stir to dissolve the sugar. Bring to a boil. Remove from the heat, add the bourbon whiskey, and stir to combine. Pour the cream mixture over the chocolate, then stir with a whisk until smooth. Pour the mixture (now ganache) onto a baking sheet with sides and spread evenly to the edges of the sheet. Refrigerate for 20 to 30 minutes until chilled but not firm.

Remove the ganache from the refrigerator. Place the butter in the bowl of an electric mixer fitted with a paddle. Mix on low speed for 1 minute, then increase the speed to medium and beat for 2 minutes until soft. Scrape down the sides of the bowl and the paddle. Beat on medium for 2 more minutes until very soft. Scrape down the sides of the bowl and the paddle. Add the chilled ganache and beat on medium for 1 minute. Again scrape down the sides of the bowl and the paddle. Beat on medium for 20 more seconds. Remove the bowl from the mixer and use a rubber spatula to finish mixing the buttercream until thoroughly combined. Transfer ¾ cup of buttercream to a pastry bag fitted with a large star tip and set aside.

ASSEMBLE THE CAKE Remove the cake triangles from the refrigerator. Place one of the complete triangles on an inverted baking sheet (make certain the baking sheet is clean and dry). Use an offset spatula to spread ⅓ cup of buttercream evenly and smoothly over the top and to the edges of the triangle. Place 2 of the half triangles (so as to form a complete triangle) on the buttercream-coated triangle and gently press into place. Now coat this layer with buttercream, then continue to stack and coat with buttercream each remaining triangle finishing the stack of 8 cake triangles with a complete triangle. Spread the remaining buttercream (not what was reserved in the pastry bag) evenly and smoothly over the top and back of the triangular cake. Pipe a row of 4 big-ass stars of buttercream (each one touching the next) along the outside edge of the top of the cake. Refrigerate for 2 to 3 hours until cold and firm.

TO SERVE This colossal cake may be served as is or cut into many pieces. I suggest using a serrated slicer to trim ⅛ inch or so from the unfrosted sides of the cake. This will make the cake appear to be a single slice cut from a big-ass cake. Because of the unusual shape of the uncut cake, I will leave how to cut it up to you.

THE CHEF'S TOUCH

If you are not enchanted with bourbon, substitute your favorite scotch or other spirit. If you prefer your cake spirit free, you can omit the bourbon without otherwise altering the recipe.

For best results, do not skimp on the maple syrup. Purchase the best—100% pure U.S. Grade A dark amber syrup.

This cake may be prepared over 2 days.

DAY 1: Bake the Chocolate Brown Sugar and Bourbon Cake layers. Four to five minutes after the cake layers have been removed from the oven, remove them from the baking sheets and cut each as directed in the recipe. Cover the triangular cake pieces with plastic wrap and refrigerate.

DAY 2: Prepare the Chocolate Bourbon Buttercream. Spread the cake triangles with the buttercream and assemble the cake as described in the recipe. Refrigerate for 2 to 3 hours before serving.

After assembly, keep the cake in the refrigerator for 2 to 3 days before serving. To avoid permeating the cake with refrigerator odors, cover the unfrosted sides with large sheets of plastic wrap.

DOUBLE DOWN DOMINO CAKES

I have enjoyed playing a game called Matadors with dominoes since my student days at the Culinary Institute of America. I taught my wife, Connie, the game on a summer vacation at the beach soon after we were married. Seems as though Connie has a knack for such things, and in short order, student became master. As a poor loser I didn't take well to her mastery, until I noticed that the ivory on some of the key blocks had distinctive markings. Guess what? She still managed to beat me more often than not. Double down your dominoes with these. Diminutive Irish Cream–enhanced chocolate cakes are bathed in dark chocolate ganache and numbered with white chocolate counterfeits, but the taste is the real thing.

MAKE THE CHOCOLATE IRISH CREAM CAKE Preheat the oven to 325°F. Lightly coat the insides of each of 16 individual nonstick petite loaf pans with the melted butter. Flour the insides of the pans with the 2 tablespoons of flour. Shake out and discard the excess flour (to prevent a mess, do this over a sink or large trash receptacle). Set aside.

In a sifter combine the ½ cup flour, the baking powder, and salt. Sift onto a large piece of parchment paper (or wax paper) and set aside.

Melt the semisweet chocolate, unsweetened chocolate, and 2 ounces butter in the top half of a double boiler, or in a small glass bowl in a microwave oven (see pages 20–21) and stir until smooth.

Place the sugar and eggs in the bowl of an electric mixer fitted with a paddle. Beat on medium-high speed for 3 minutes until light in color and slightly thickened. Add the chocolate and butter mixture and mix on low speed to combine, about 20 seconds. Operate the mixer on low while gradually adding the dry ingredients. Once all the dry ingredients have been incorporated, about 40 seconds, stop the mixer and scrape down the sides of the bowl. Add the Irish Cream and mix on low for

CHOCOLATE IRISH CREAM CAKE

1 tablespoon unsalted butter, melted

2 ounces unsalted butter, cut into ½-ounce pieces

½ cup all-purpose flour plus 2 tablespoons

1 teaspoon baking powder

½ teaspoon salt

3 ounces semisweet baking chocolate, coarsely chopped

2 ounces unsweetened baking chocolate, coarsely chopped

¾ cup granulated sugar

3 large eggs

¼ cup Baileys Original Irish Cream

¾ cup semisweet chocolate mini-morsels

BAILEYS CHOCOLATE GANACHE

6 ounces semisweet baking chocolate, coarsely chopped

2 ounces unsweetened
chocolate, coarsely
chopped
1 cup heavy cream
2 ounces unsalted butter, cut
into ½-ounce pieces
2 tablespoons Baileys
Original Irish Cream
1 tablespoon granulated
sugar

MELTED WHITE CHOCOLATE
GARNISH
2 ounces white chocolate,
coarsely chopped and
melted (see pages 20–21)

MAKES 16 DOMINOS

15 seconds (the batter has a good-enough-to-eat chocolaty color, but resist the temptation and prevent internal fluctuation). Remove the bowl from the mixer and use a rubber spatula to fold in the mini-morsels and finish mixing the batter until thoroughly combined.

Pour 3 slightly heaping tablespoons or 1 slightly heaping #20 ice cream scoop (about 1½ ounces) into each loaf pan. (The batter is liquid enough not to need spreading, although a wiggle while you walk to the oven will not hurt.)

Place the pans on the top and center racks of the oven and bake until a toothpick inserted in the center of one of the cakes comes out clean, about 14 minutes. (Rotate the pans from top to center halfway through the baking time, and turn each 180 degrees.) Remove the cakes from the oven and cool in the pans at room temperature for 5 minutes.

Place 2 cooling racks onto 2 baking sheets with sides. Invert the pans to release the cakes onto the racks. (If the cakes do not pop out of the pans, use a small plastic knife to cut around the edges of the cakes to free them from the pans without tearing.) Put 8 cakes, evenly spaced, onto each cooling rack and refrigerate.

PREPARE THE BAILEYS CHOCOLATE GANACHE Place the chopped chocolate and unsweetened chocolate in a medium bowl.

Heat the heavy cream, butter, Irish Cream, and sugar in a small saucepan over medium-high heat. When hot, stir to dissolve the sugar. Bring to a boil. Pour the boiling cream over the chocolate, then stir with a whisk until smooth.

COAT THE CAKES WITH GANACHE Remove a pan with 8 of the cakes from the refrigerator. Cover each cake with 2 ounces (4 tablespoons) of ganache, allowing the ganache to flow over the top and sides of each cake. Transfer the rack of ganache-coated cakes to the refrigerator. Use a rubber spatula to remove the ganache from the baking sheet, return it to the bowl of ganache (stir gently until smooth), and use as necessary to cover each cake on the second pan with 2 ounces of ganache (you probably will have to scrape ganache from the baking sheet after coating 6 of the cakes. Place the cakes in the refrigerator for 20 minutes. (Now use a spoon to convey any leftover ganache from the baking sheet to an eager mouth.)

NUMBER THE DOMINOES WITH THE WHITE CHOCOLATE GARNISH, THEN PLAY THE GAME Place the white chocolate in a small plastic zippered bag. Snip the tip from a bottom corner of the bag. Pipe a line of white chocolate across the center of each cake, then pipe from 1 to 6 dots on either side of the line. Refrigerate for at least 15 minutes before serving.

*T*HE CHEF'S TOUCH

The nonstick petite loaf pans can be found at your local Target or other major discount or kitchen emporium. Each pan holds ⅔ cup and is 4 × 2¾ × 1½ inches.

For quicker and more efficient portioning of the Chocolate Irish Cream Cake batter, use a #20 ice cream scoop rather than a measuring spoon, and pour a level scoop into each individual petite loaf pan.

At The Trellis, pastry chef Kelly Bailey uses 12-ounce clear plastic squeeze bottles for decorating with white chocolate. For the small amount of white chocolate needed for the dominoes, we decided to use a plastic zippered bag (we snipped the corner and used it like a pastry bag). Squeeze bottles are handier and can be purchased at kitchenware stores, or you can also use ketchup or mustard squeeze bottles.

These cakes may be prepared over 2 days.

DAY 1: Bake the individual Chocolate Irish Cream Cakes. Once cooled, cover with plastic wrap and refrigerate until assembling the dominoes (the cakes may be kept covered in the refrigerator for several days before assembly, or frozen for 2 to 3 weeks).

DAY 2: Make the Baileys Chocolate Ganache, cover the cakes with ganache, then refrigerate while melting the white chocolate. Transform the cakes into dominoes by garnishing with the white chocolate. Refrigerate for 15 minutes before serving.

Once they are assembled, you may keep the cakes in the refrigerator for 3 to 4 days before serving. To avoid permeating the dominoes with refrigerator odors, place them in a large, tightly sealed plastic container.

WHITE CHOCOLATE PUMPKIN CHEESECAKES WITH BLACKBERRY PIXILATION

WALNUT CORN FLAKES
CRUST

5 cups corn flakes

1½ cups walnuts, toasted
(see page 23)

½ cup (4 ounces) tightly
packed dark brown sugar

5 tablespoons unsalted
butter, melted

WHITE CHOCOLATE
PUMPKIN CHEESECAKES

10 ounces cream cheese, cut
into 1-ounce pieces

¾ cup (6 ounces) tightly
packed light brown sugar

½ teaspoon salt

6 ounces white chocolate,
coarsely chopped and
melted (see pages 20–21)

4 large eggs

½ cup 100% natural solid-
pack pumpkin

1 teaspoon pure vanilla
extract

Halloween promotes odd behavior. The service staff at The Trellis always seizes the opportunity to transform themselves for the occasion. They have appeared in creative garb—mermaid, ax murderer, Mother Hubbard with her shoe, a peanut M&M, etc. Our pastry chef Kelly Bailey is always challenged by the sartorial excesses to come up with a dessert that fits the spirit. How about this? A crispy toasted walnut and golden corn flakes crust, framing a velvety pumpkin cheesecake enriched with white chocolate. Ladle on red wine-soaked blackberries and your spirits will soar.

MAKE THE WALNUT CORN FLAKES CRUST Assemble six 4 × 1½-inch nonstick springform pans with the bottom insert turned over (the lip of the insert facing down).

Place the corn flakes in the bowl of a food processor fitted with a metal blade. Pulse the flakes until they have a medium-fine texture, about 45 seconds. Add the walnuts to the bowl and pulse until fine, about 30 seconds. Add the brown sugar and butter and pulse for 20 seconds. Portion ½ cup (about 2½ ounces) of the crust mixture into each springform pan. One pan at a time, use your fingers to evenly and firmly press the crust mixture onto the bottom and sides of the pan. (The crust mixture should reach the rim of the pan.) Set aside while preparing the cheesecake batter.

MAKE THE WHITE CHOCOLATE PUMPKIN CHEESECAKES Preheat the oven to 325°F.

Place the cream cheese, brown sugar, and salt in the bowl of an electric mixer fitted with a paddle. Mix on low for 1 minute; then beat on medium-high speed for 4 minutes until soft and thoroughly combined. Use a rubber spatula to scrape down the sides of the bowl and the paddle. Add the white chocolate and mix on medium to combine, about 15 seconds. Add the eggs, one at a time, beating on medium for 30 seconds after each addition, and scraping down the sides of the bowl once all the eggs have been incorporated. Add the pumpkin and vanilla extract and beat on medium to combine, about 20 seconds. At this point the batter has a pleasingly pale pumpkin patina. Remove the bowl from the mixer and use a rubber spatula to finish mixing the ingredients until thoroughly combined.

Portion ¾ cup (about 5 ounces) of batter into each crust-lined springform pan. Place the pans on a baking sheet. Place the baking sheet on the center rack of the oven and bake for 20 minutes. Lower the oven temperature to 225°F and bake until the internal temperature of the cheesecake reaches 170°F, about 55 minutes (the cheesecakes will also be firm to the touch and have slightly domed tops). Remove the cheesecakes from the oven and cool at room temperature in the pans for 20 minutes. (While cooling, the tops of the cakes will collapse very slightly, creating a small recession that will be filled with the Blackberry Pixilation.) Refrigerate the cheesecakes for 3 hours before unmolding.

PREPARE THE BLACKBERRY PIXILATION Place the blackberries and their juices in a noncorrosive medium bowl.

Heat the wine and brown sugar in a medium saucepan over medium heat. When hot, stir to dissolve the sugar. Bring to a boil, then adjust the heat and allow to simmer for 23 to 24 minutes until thickened to the consistency of a light syrup. Remove from the heat. Pour the hot syrup over the blackberries in the bowl. Stir gently to cover the blackberries with the syrup. The powerful perfume of this mixture is irresistible. If you are so inclined, I suggest tasting these berries—ah, promises of things to come. Transfer the berries to a baking sheet with sides and refrigerate until cold. Once the berries are cold, return them to the noncorrosive bowl, cover with plastic wrap, and refrigerate.

TO SERVE Remove the cakes from the refrigerator. Release the cakes from the springform pans. Use a small spatula to remove the cakes from the bottom inserts of the pans. Spoon 2 heaping tablespoons of the chilled berries and juices into the recession on the top of each cake. Serve immediately.

BLACKBERRY PIXILATION

2½ cups frozen blackberries, thawed

1½ cups red table wine

½ cup (4 ounces) tightly packed light brown sugar

MAKES 6 INDIVIDUAL CAKES

THE CHEF'S TOUCH

The subtle sweet flavor of pumpkin is enhanced by other ingredients, which is why so many cooks are tempted to overseason it. In this dessert, the white chocolate does not overwhelm the pumpkin. There's no reason to insist on using fresh pumpkin when only ¾ cup is called for. So I give in—this time—and recommend canned 100% natural solid-pack pumpkin. Make certain you check the label on the canned pumpkin so that you do not mistakenly purchase pumpkin pie filling, which is tangled by too many tongue-tingling spices.

The uniquely sized 4 × 1½-inch nonstick springform pans used in this recipe are available from Wilton Enterprises (see Online Sources, page 161). Wilton calls the pans Singles!, I call them fun. Even though the pans are manufactured to last for many years, they are inexpensive.

Turning over the bottom inserts of the springform pans (with the lip of the bottom inserts facing down) before assembling the pans will make it easier to remove the finished desserts from the bottoms of the pans.

To thaw the blackberries quickly, place them in a medium glass bowl. Place the bowl in a microwave oven set on defrost for 3½ minutes. Remove the bowl from the microwave, then stir the berries gently. Return the berries to the microwave for 3½ more minutes on defrost. Set aside at room temperature.

The most accurate way to measure the internal temperature of the cheesecake is by using an instant-read thermometer.

Perhaps you don't fancy blackberries. Consider frozen red raspberries in their place (use the same directions as for the blackberries).

After assembly, you keep the cheesecakes in the refrigerator for 2 days before serving. To avoid exposing the cakes to odorous refrigerator vapors, place them in a large, tightly sealed plastic container. The Blackberry Pixilation will keep for several days stored in a noncorrosive container in the refrigerator. This dessert may be prepared over 3 days.

DAY 1: Prepare and refrigerate the Blackberry Pixilation, covered in a noncorrosive bowl.

DAY 2: Make the Walnut Corn Flakes Crust. Make and bake the White Chocolate Pumpkin Cheesecakes. Cool to room temperature, then refrigerate.

DAY 3: Remove the cakes from the refrigerator. Release from the springform pans. Serve with the blackberries as directed in the recipe.

COCOA CINNAMON CHOCOLATE CHIP SHORTCAKES

These bite-size cocoa and cinnamon–enhanced shortcakes are just the item to serve at an afternoon tea. Garnish each shortcake with a dollop of whipped cream and the elegant morsels are ready to be devoured with delight.

Preheat the oven to 350°F.

Place a seasoned cast-iron, 12-mold, fluted mini-muffin pan in the oven for 15 minutes. Remove the pan from the oven. (Handle with care—cast iron retains a lot of heat.) Use a pastry brush to lightly brush the insides of each fluted mold in the pan with some of the vegetable oil. Set aside at room temperature while preparing the shortcake batter.

In a sifter combine the flour, sugar, cocoa powder, baking powder, cinnamon, and salt. Sift directly into the bowl of an electric mixer. Position the bowl onto the electric mixer, then fit with a paddle. Mix on the lowest speed (stir) to combine the dry ingredients, about 15 seconds. Add the butter and mix on the lowest speed until the butter is cut into the dry ingredients and the mixture develops a very coarse texture, about 1½ minutes. Continue to operate the mixer on the lowest speed while gradually adding the buttermilk. Once the buttermilk has been incorporated, about 15 seconds (the batter appears very grainy at this point), add the chocolate mini-morsels and mix on medium for 10 seconds to combine. Remove the bowl from the mixer and use a rubber spatula to finish mixing the batter until thoroughly combined.

Portion 2 slightly heaping tablespoons (a bit more than 1½ ounces) or 1 slightly heaping #30 ice cream scoop of the shortcake batter into each mold. Place the pan on the center rack of the oven and bake until a toothpick inserted in the center of one of the cakes comes out clean, about 27 minutes. Remove the shortcakes from the oven and cool at

1 teaspoon vegetable oil

1 cup all-purpose flour

¼ cup granulated sugar

2 tablespoons unsweetened cocoa powder

1¼ teaspoons baking powder

½ teaspoon ground cinnamon

¼ teaspoon salt

3 ounces unsalted butter, cut into ½-ounce pieces

¾ cup buttermilk

½ cup semisweet chocolate mini-morsels

MAKES 12 SHORTCAKES

room temperature for 10 minutes. Invert the pan to release the cakes. Serve immediately or set aside at room temperature until ready to serve.

*T*HE CHEF'S TOUCH

We found the cast-iron, 12-mold, fluted mini-muffin pan at the legendary Williamsburg Pottery, a shrine for pilgrims from across America. Located just a few miles from the center of Williamsburg, the Pottery has everything from kitsch statuary to practical cookware. If you are not planning a trip to Williamsburg (you should be), look for this particular pan in your local kitchenware or hardware store.

The cast-iron, 12-mold, fluted mini-muffin pan must be seasoned before use. First, wash the pan with warm soapy water. Never, ever scour the pan with an abrasive pad. Thoroughly rinse then dry the pan. Lightly brush the insides of each fluted mold in the pan with vegetable oil. Place the pan in a preheated 350°F oven for 1 hour. Remove the now seasoned pan from the oven and cool to room temperature before storing. After using the pan, use paper towels to wipe the insides clean, then brush the insides of each fluted mold in the pan with a very thin coating of oil (to prevent rusting) before storing. If necessary, you can wash the pan using hot water, but don't use an abrasive pad.

For a stylish and light dessert, serve 2 shortcakes with fresh fruit puree and a spoonful or two of whipped cream (consider enhancing the cream with ground cinnamon).

The shortcakes may be held at room temperature for several hours before serving. They may be served at room temperature or warm. To serve warm, place one or two shortcakes at a time in a microwave oven set on medium for 10 seconds. The shortcakes may also be refrigerated for 24 hours stored in a tightly sealed plastic container, then warmed in a microwave oven.

HOT CHOCOLATE
SNOW DAY CAKES

Snow days were a regular event when I was growing up in New England. I fondly remember how good it felt not to have to walk to school on those wet and cold days, but it was not the exercise I minded, which was evidenced by the number of driveways that I and a few other of my entrepreneurial friends managed to liberate from winter's snowy deposit. What I most clearly remember was that at the end of the shoveling day, mom always had a pot of hot chocolate and a chocolate confection awaiting. Each of these pint-size confections is topped with a cap of cool whipped cocoa cream that is bound to melt away winter cares.

MAKE THE HOT CHOCOLATE Heat the milk, sugar, vanilla extract, and almond extract in a medium saucepan over medium heat. When hot, stir to dissolve the sugar. Bring to a simmer. Add the chopped semisweet chocolate and stir with a whisk until the chocolate has melted. Remove from the heat and set aside.

MAKE THE HOT CHOCOLATE SNOW DAY CAKES Preheat the oven to 325°F. Lightly coat the insides of each of 16 individual nonstick petite loaf pans with the melted butter. Flour the insides of the pans with the 2 tablespoons flour. Shake out and discard the excess flour. Set aside.

In a sifter combine the 2¼ cups flour, the cocoa powder, baking powder, and baking soda. Sift onto a large piece of parchment paper (or wax paper) and set aside until needed.

Place the ½ pound butter and the sugar in the bowl of an electric mixer fitted with a paddle. Mix on low speed for 1 minute, then beat on medium until soft, about 2 minutes. Scrape down the sides of the bowl and the paddle. Beat for an additional 2 minutes on medium until very soft. Scrape down the sides of the bowl and the paddle. Add the eggs, one at a time, beating on medium for 30 seconds after each addition, and

HOT CHOCOLATE
- ¾ cup whole milk
- ¼ cup granulated sugar
- ½ teaspoon pure vanilla extract
- ¼ teaspoon pure almond extract
- 2 ounces semisweet baking chocolate, coarsely chopped

SNOW DAY CAKES
- 1 tablespoon unsalted butter, melted
- ½ pound (2 sticks) unsalted butter, cut into ¼-ounce pieces
- 2¼ cups all-purpose flour plus 2 tablespoons
- ¼ cup unsweetened cocoa powder
- 1 teaspoon baking powder
- ¾ teaspoon baking soda
- 1 cup granulated sugar
- 3 large eggs

COCOA SNOW CAP CREAM

1½ cups heavy cream

⅓ cup confectioners' sugar
    plus 3 tablespoons

2 tablespoons unsweetened
    cocoa powder

MAKES 16 CAKES

scraping down the sides of the bowl once all the eggs have been incorporated. Operate the mixer on the lowest speed (stir) while gradually adding the dry ingredients. Once they have been incorporated, about 1½ minutes, gradually add the hot chocolate and mix until incorporated, about 45 seconds. Scrape down the sides of the bowl and the paddle. Beat on medium for 20 seconds until thoroughly combined. Remove the bowl from the mixer and use a rubber spatula to finish mixing the ingredients until thoroughly combined.

Portion ⅓ cup (a little less than 3 ounces) or 2 slightly heaping #30 ice cream scoops into each pan. No need to spread the batter, as it will spread on its own in the oven.

Place the pans on the top and center racks of the oven and bake until a toothpick inserted in the center of one of the cakes comes out clean, 25 to 26 minutes. (Rotate the pans from top to center halfway through the baking time, and turn each 180 degrees.) Remove the cakes from the oven and cool in the pan for 5 minutes at room temperature.

Invert the pans to release the cakes. (If the cakes do not pop out of the pans, hold the pans upside down and tap an edge on the countertop—the cakes should just pop right out). Set the cakes aside while preparing the Cocoa Snow Cap Cream.

PREPARE THE COCOA SNOW CAP CREAM AND ENJOY THE SNOW DAY   Place the heavy cream, ⅓ cup confectioners' sugar, and the cocoa powder in the bowl of an electric mixer fitted with a balloon whip. Whisk the mixture on medium speed for 10 seconds, then whisk on medium-high until soft peaks form, about 1 minute.

TO SERVE   Use the smooth side of teaspoon to press a small indentation into the top of each cake. Spoon 2 to 3 slightly heaping tablespoons of the Cocoa Snow Cap Cream into each of the cakes. Dust the cakes with the remaining 3 tablespoons confectioners' sugar and serve immediately.

𝒯HE CHEF'S TOUCH

The nonstick petite loaf pans can be found at your local Target or other major discount or kitchen emporium. Each loaf pan holds ⅔ cup and is 4 × 2¾ × 1½ inches.

The Hot Chocolate Snow Day Cakes are best when served warm. Once they're cooled to room temperature, store them for 3 to 4 days at room temperature in a tightly sealed plastic container. Room-temperature cakes may be warmed in a microwave. Warming them takes 10 to 15 seconds on defrost in our 1100-watt microwave at Ganache Hill. It may take you a few seconds more or less in your microwave, depending upon the wattage.

You can double or even quadruple our Hot Chocolate recipe and offer that beverage along with the cakes, or, if it's an adult crowd that is snowed in, go for the Hot Chocolate Buccaneer (page 160).

COOKIES

Behold a stunning array of chocolate handheld treats
that run the gamut of chocoholic delight. From the
alluring molasses-laced Chocolate Shoofly Bites
to the dangerously dark Black Mamba Cookies,
every munch brings explosions of flavor and
mouth-watering pleasure.

Chocolate Peanut Butter and Jelly Sandwich Cookies

These fanciful sandwich cookies fool the eye. Two pieces of "bread," made from cookie dough, are held together with peanut butter and grape jelly—a sandwich for kids of all ages. A glass of cold milk is the only possible accompaniment.

MAKE THE WHITE CHOCOLATE BREAD DOUGH In a sifter combine the flour and salt. Sift onto a large piece of parchment paper (or wax paper) and set aside.

Place the butter and sugar in the bowl of an electric mixer fitted with a paddle. Mix on low speed for 1 minute; then beat on medium for 2 minutes until soft. Use a rubber spatula to scrape down the sides of the bowl and the paddle. Add the egg and beat on medium for 1 minute. Scrape down the sides of the bowl. Add the white chocolate and mix on medium for 20 seconds. Operate the mixer on low while gradually adding the dry ingredients; mix until incorporated, about 1 minute. Scrape down the sides of the bowl and the paddle. Mix on medium speed for an additional 10 seconds. (Usually, I would ask you to use a rubber spatula to finish mixing the ingredients until thoroughly combined. But as this dough is very stiff, the mixing on medium for the additional 10 seconds will do the task more thoroughly than the rubber spatula.)

Transfer the dough to a 12 × 12-inch piece of parchment paper (or wax paper). Use your hands (the dough is a bit sticky and buttery, so you may want to wear a pair of disposable vinyl or latex gloves) to form the dough into a rectangle 8 inches long, 2½ inches wide, and 2 inches high. Now form the rectangle into a shape that resembles a loaf of bread (flat on the bottom and sides and rounded at the top). Fold the excess paper, one side at a time, over the loaf, then place on a baking sheet and refrigerate until needed.

WHITE CHOCOLATE BREAD DOUGH

2¼ cups all-purpose flour

½ teaspoon salt

½ pound (2 sticks) unsalted butter, cut into ½-ounce pieces

1 cup granulated sugar

1 large egg

3 ounces white chocolate, coarsely chopped and melted (see pages 20–21)

CHOCOLATE CRUST DOUGH

1 cup all-purpose flour

⅛ teaspoon salt

3 ounces unsalted butter, cut into ½-ounce pieces

½ cup granulated sugar

1 large egg white

1 ounce unsweetened baking chocolate, coarsely chopped and melted (see pages 20–21)

PEANUT BUTTER AND JELLY

¹⁄₃ cup (4 ounces) creamy
    peanut butter

¹⁄₃ cup (4¹⁄₄ ounces) grape
    jelly

MAKES 16 SANDWICHES

MAKE THE CHOCOLATE CRUST DOUGH   In a sifter combine the flour and salt. Sift onto a large piece of parchment paper (or wax paper) and set aside until needed.

Place the butter and sugar in the bowl of an electric mixer fitted with a paddle. Mix on low speed for 1 minute, then beat on medium for 2 minutes until soft. Scrape down the sides of the bowl and the paddle. Add the egg white and beat on medium for 1 minute. Scrape down the sides of the bowl. Add the unsweetened chocolate and mix on medium for 20 seconds. Operate the mixer on low while gradually adding the sifted dry ingredients; mix until incorporated, about 45 seconds. Scrape down the sides of the bowl and the paddle. Mix on medium speed for an additional 10 seconds. Transfer the dough to a 12 × 18-inch piece of parchment paper (or wax paper). Use your hands to form the dough into a rectangle 6 inches long, 3 inches wide, and 1 inch thick. Fold the excess paper, one side at a time, over the dough, then place on a baking sheet and refrigerate for 1 hour.

FINISH ASSEMBLING AND BAKE THE DOUGH LOAF   Remove the chocolate crust dough from the refrigerator and place it on a dry work surface. Fold back the excess paper from the dough, leaving the dough on the paper. Position another piece of 12 × 18-inch paper over the top of the dough. Use a rolling pin to roll the dough into a rectangle about 10 inches wide, 14 inches long, and ¹⁄₄ inch thick. If you end up with something a little larger, not to worry—as long as the rectangle is at least 10 × 14 inches, it will work as planned. Slowly remove the paper from the top of the rolled dough and discard.

Remove the white chocolate dough loaf from the refrigerator. Discard the paper. Place the loaf lengthwise in the center and across the width of the chocolate crust dough (the ends of the loaf should almost touch the edges of the chocolate crust dough). Fold one side of the crust dough up and over, then gently press the chocolate crust into the loaf. Now pull the paper away from the very top of the crust-covered loaf (don't pull the paper all the way down to the sides). Fold the other side of the crust dough up and over the loaf. Fold the paper back over the top of the loaf. Use your hand to gently but firmly press the crust dough into the sides and top of the loaf. If the crust dough is not flat against the loaf, air pockets may form. Refrigerate for at least 1 hour.

Preheat the oven to 325°F.

Remove the chilled loaf from the refrigerator and place on a clean, dry cutting board. Remove and discard the paper. Use a serrated slicer to trim the excess chocolate crust dough from each end of the loaf (so that each end is flat.) Cut the loaf into 32 slices, each ¼ inch thick. Divide the slices among 4 nonstick baking sheets.

Place 1 baking sheet on the top rack and 1 baking sheet on the center rack of the oven and bake for 15 to 16 minutes, rotating the sheets from top to center halfway through the baking time (at that time also turn each sheet 180 degrees). The remaining 2 baking sheets may be placed in another 325°F oven or held at room temperature, then baked after the first 2 sheets are removed from the oven. Remove the cookies from the oven and cool to room temperature on the baking sheets, about 20 minutes.

FINISH ASSEMBLING THE CHOCOLATE PEANUT BUTTER AND JELLY SANDWICH COOKIES After the cookie "bread" slices have cooled, use a small offset spatula (or butter knife) to spread 2 teaspoons of the peanut butter on 16 of the slices. Use a clean offset spatula to spread 2 teaspoons of the jelly onto the remaining 16 slices of cookie bread. Gently press one of the peanut butter–spread cookies together with one of the jelly-spread cookies. Repeat with the remaining peanut butter and jelly–spread cookies until you have 16 sandwiches. Cut each sandwich in half. Store in a tightly sealed plastic container in the refrigerator.

𝒯HE CHEF'S TOUCH

The assembled cookies will keep for several days in the refrigerator if stored in a tightly sealed plastic container. The slices of unassembled baked cookies (without the peanut butter and jelly) may be stored for up to several weeks in the freezer. Be certain to place them in a tightly sealed plastic container to prevent dehydration and protect them from freezer odors.

Granny's Chocolate-and-Walnut-Covered Coffee-Cocoa Marshmallow Squares

COFFEE-COCOA MARSHMALLOWS

1 teaspoon vegetable oil

1½ tablespoons confectioners' sugar

1½ tablespoons cornstarch

1½ cup unsweetened cocoa powder

1 cup brewed full-strength hot coffee

3 packages (¾ ounce) unflavored granulated gelatin

2 tablespoons coffee liqueur

1½ cups granulated sugar

1 tablespoon light corn syrup

2 large egg whites

1 tablespoon pure vanilla extract

According to Ganache Hill test kitchen chef Brett Bailey, the most excellent marshmallow of all time was perfected by his Granny Bailey. Unfortunately, Granny Bailey was a bit more than circumspect when it came to sharing a recipe, let alone passing on the secret of her justly beloved marshmallows. Don't despair; the spirit of Granny Bailey lives on with Brett's interpretation of a mallow that is moist, dense, and boldly flavored with coffee and cocoa, then bathed in chocolate. Granny doesn't need a brand new bag—she's got her marshmallow squares.

MAKE THE COFFEE-COCOA MARSHMALLOWS Lightly coat the inside of a 9 × 9 × 1½-inch nonstick cake pan with the vegetable oil. In a sifter combine 1 tablespoon of the confectioners' sugar and 1 tablespoon of the cornstarch. Sift directly into the prepared pan, coating the entire bottom of the pan. Shake the pan to coat the sides uniformly, then gently shake out any excess. Set aside.

Place the cocoa powder in a sifter and sift onto a large piece of parchment paper (or wax paper) and set aside.

Place ¼ cup of the coffee, the gelatin, and the coffee liqueur in the top half of a double boiler over medium-low heat. Stir to combine and dissolve the gelatin. Keep the mixture in the double boiler over low heat.

Heat the granulated sugar, the remaining ¾ cup coffee, and the corn syrup in a large saucepan over medium-high heat. When hot, stir to dissolve the sugar. Bring to a boil. Boil the mixture until it reaches a temperature of 260°F, 10 to 11 minutes (the mixture will get very frothy and appear as if it will boil out of the saucepan; relax—as long as you used a large saucepan, the mixture will be contained). Be certain to use a candy thermometer versus an instant-read thermometer for an accurate temperature reading of the hot mixture. Remove from the heat. Use a wire whisk to rapidly stir the mixture until the froth has dissipated. Slowly add the hot coffee and gelatin mixture. Continue whisking until combined, about 1 minute.

Place the egg whites in the bowl of an electric mixer fitted with a balloon whip. Whisk on high until frothy, about 45 seconds. Gradually add the very hot sugar and coffee mixture to the frothy egg whites in a slow, steady stream while whisking on high until the very hot mixture is incorporated, about 1 minute. Continue to whisk on high for an additional 7 minutes until fluffy but almost firm in texture. Now operate the mixer on the lowest speed (stir) while gradually adding the sifted cocoa powder (the mixer will labor to operate because the mixture is so thick). Once the cocoa powder has been incorporated, about 40 seconds, stop the mixer and scrape down the sides of the bowl. Add the vanilla extract and mix on low for 10 seconds. Increase the speed of the mixer to high and whisk for an additional 30 seconds until the mixture is a uniform light brown. Transfer the mixture to the prepared pan, using a rubber spatula to spread it evenly to the edges of the pan (this takes a wee bit of effort because of the extreme stickiness of the mixture).

In a sifter combine the remaining ½ tablespoon confectioners' sugar and ½ tablespoon cornstarch; sift directly over the entire top of the marshmallow mixture in the pan. Set aside at room temperature until fairly firm to the touch, about 1 hour.

Use a pastry brush to brush off as much of the sifted ingredients as possible from the top of the marshmallow. Use a sharp, thin-bladed paring knife to carefully cut the marshmallow away from the sides of the pan. Invert the marshmallow square onto a clean, dry work surface. Use a pastry brush to dust off as much of the sifted ingredients as possible from the inverted surface of the marshmallow. Use a sharp knife to cut the marshmallow square in half, then cut each of those pieces in half lengthwise, creating 4 equal-size strips. Continue by cutting each strip into 4 equal-size pieces. This will yield 16 squares. Set aside.

FINISH THE COFFEE-COCOA MARSHMALLOW SQUARES Line a baking sheet with parchment paper (or wax paper).

CHOCOLATE AND WALNUT COATING

¾ pound bittersweet baking chocolate, coarsely chopped and melted (see pages 20–21)

¼ cup walnut pieces, toasted (see page 23) and coarsely chopped

MAKES 16 SQUARES

Wearing a pair of disposable vinyl (or latex) gloves, dip each marsh-mallow square, one at a time, briefly into the melted bittersweet choco-late, turning the square to entirely coat it with chocolate. Place the chocolate-coated square on the parchment-lined baking sheet. Once all of the squares have been coated in chocolate, sprinkle the top of each with ½ teaspoon chopped walnuts. Return to a baking sheet lined with clean parchment paper (or wax paper) and refrigerate for 30 minutes to harden the chocolate before serving.

𝒯HE CHEF'S TOUCH

I like the color highlight and the depth of flavor achieved by using bittersweet baking chocolate as a covering for the marshmallow squares. It's no problem, however, to substitute semisweet chocolate. Use the same amount and follow the directions as stated in the recipe for bittersweet.

The marshmallows may be prepared and garnished over 2 days.

DAY 1: Make the Coffee-Cocoa Marshmallows as directed in the recipe. Once the marshmallow mixture has cooled in the pan at room tempera-ture for 1 hour and is firm to the touch, cover the pan with plastic wrap and set aside at room temperature until the next day (in fact, you could keep the marshmallow in the plastic wrap–covered pan at room temper-ature for 3 to 4 days before proceeding).

DAY 2: Remove the 9-inch square from the pan as directed, then cut into 16 squares. Coat with chocolate and walnuts, then refrigerate for 30 minutes before serving.

Consider cutting the Coffee-Cocoa Marshmallow Square into smaller, bite-size portions. They can be gobbled up with or without the chocolate-walnut coating. Uncoated marshmallow pieces are a worthy addition to a cup of hot chocolate; that should get you all marshmal-lowy.

CHOCOLATE SHOOFLY BITES

Dark as a starless night, bold with the caramel tones of molasses, yet buttery and chocolate at the same time—our interpretation of shoofly pie may seem impious—and it is!

MAKE THE CHOCOLATE BUTTER CRUST Preheat the oven to 350°F. Lightly coat the inside of a 10¾ × 7 × 1½-inch nonstick biscuit/brownie pan with the melted butter. Set aside.

Sift the all-purpose flour onto a large piece of parchment paper (or wax paper) and set aside.

Place the 3 ounces butter and the sugar in the bowl of an electric mixer fitted with a paddle. Mix on low speed for 1 minute; then beat on medium for 1 minute until slightly soft. Use a rubber spatula to scrape down the sides of the bowl and the paddle. Add the egg yolk and beat on medium for 1 minute until combined. Scrape down the sides of the bowl and the paddle. Add the semisweet chocolate and beat on medium for 15 seconds until incorporated. Scrape down the sides of the bowl and the paddle. Operate the mixer on low while gradually adding the sifted flour; mix until incorporated, about 40 seconds. Scrape down the sides of the bowl and the paddle. Now mix on medium for 10 seconds until the dough is a uniform light chocolate color. Transfer the dough to the prepared pan. Wearing a pair of disposable vinyl (or latex) gloves, evenly press the dough into the bottom of the pan from the center to the edges in a uniform thickness (this will not be difficult as the dough is very soft). Use a flat, nonperforated spatula to press down on the dough to eliminate finger indentations.

Using the tines of a fork, prick the dough in the bottom of the pan about 100 times (it sounds like a lot of pricks, but it will only take a few seconds to accomplish) over the entire surface of the dough (this will allow steam to escape while the crust is baking).

Bake on the center rack in the oven until the dough becomes slightly puffy, about 12 minutes. Remove the partially baked crust from the oven and set aside at room temperature.

CHOCOLATE BUTTER CRUST

1 teaspoon unsalted butter, melted

3 ounces unsalted butter, cut into ¼-ounce pieces

1 cup all-purpose flour

¼ cup granulated sugar

1 large egg yolk

2 ounces semisweet baking chocolate, coarsely chopped and melted (see pages 20–21)

BROWN SUGAR CRUMBLE

1 cup all-purpose flour

¾ cup (6 ounces) tightly packed light brown sugar

¼ pound (1 stick) unsalted butter, cut into ⅛-ounce pieces

1 teaspoon baking soda

CHOCOLATE SHOOFLY CENTER

¼ cup mild flavor molasses (such as Grandma's brand unsulfured)

¼ cup light corn syrup

2 large eggs

6 ounces semisweet baking
   chocolate, coarsely
   chopped and melted
   (see pages 20–21)
⅓ cup half-and-half

MAKES 48 BITES

MAKE THE BROWN SUGAR CRUMBLE Place the flour, brown sugar, butter, and baking soda in the bowl of an electric mixer fitted with a paddle. Mix on the lowest speed (stir) for 1 minute; then mix on low for 1½ minutes until the mixture resembles coarse sand. Set aside.

MAKE THE CHOCOLATE SHOOFLY CENTER Place the molasses, corn syrup, and eggs in the bowl of an electric mixer fitted with a paddle. Beat on medium speed for 1 minute until slightly frothy. Add the semisweet chocolate and mix on medium for 30 seconds until combined. Use a rubber spatula to scrape down the sides of the bowl. Add the half-and-half and mix on low for 15 seconds. Remove the bowl from the mixer.

Add 1½ cups of the Brown Sugar Crumble, then use a rubber spatula to finish mixing the sweet and sticky batter until thoroughly combined (the batter is quite odoriferous from the agitation of the molasses, but don't be put off—remember the adage: to make an omelet you have to crack a few eggs). Pour the batter on top of the partially baked Chocolate Butter Crust (no need to spread the batter, as it is quite liquid). Sprinkle the remaining Brown Sugar Crumble onto the top of the batter. Bake on the center rack of the oven for 45 minutes until the batter does not jiggle when the pan is wiggled.

Remove the pan from the oven and allow to cool at room temperature for 20 minutes until slightly cooled. Use a sharp paring knife to cut around the edges and help release the shoofly from the pan. Invert the shoofly onto a large piece of parchment paper (or wax paper). Use this paper to help turn the shoofly over so that the baked Brown Sugar Crumble side is up. Place the shoofly on a baking sheet and refrigerate for 1 hour until cold. Use a serrated slicer to cut the shoofly into 1¼-inch squares. For a clean cut, heat the blade of the slicer under hot running water and wipe the blade dry before making each cut. To accentuate the shoofly experience, keep the bites at room temperature for about 30 minutes before serving.

𝒯HE CHEF'S TOUCH

A by-product of processing sugar cane, molasses has a specific flavor and aroma that is usually not favored by the uninitiated. Here we have toned it down by joining the molasses with light corn syrup, and additionally with chocolate. With the injection of chocolate, the shoofly has

Chocolate Hazelnut
Christmas Tree Stump

(PAGE 29)

Pretty in Pink Cake

(PAGE 33)

Mrs. D's "She Ain't Heavy" Chocolate Cake

(PAGE 36)

White Chocolate Pumpkin Cheesecakes
with Blackberry Pixilation

(PAGE 68)

*Cocoa Cinnamon
Chocolate Chip Shortcakes*

(PAGE 71)

*Chocolate Peanut Butter and Jelly
Sandwich Cookies*

(PAGE 77)

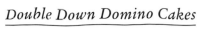

Mrs. D's "She Ain't Heavy" Chocolate Cake

(PAGE 36)

Dawn's Chocolate Cherry
Whirly-Swirly Cookies

(PAGE 99)

Caramel Orange–Chocolate Orange
Masquerade Ice Cream Terrine

(PAGE 105)

Chocolate Grasshopper
Ice Cream Sandwich

(PAGE 117)

Red, White, and Blue Berry Ice Cream

(PAGE 127)

Cocoa Mint-Julep Pop

(PAGE 129)

Cocoa Berry Yogurt Mousse

(PAGE 136)

Frozen Chocolate Oh-Honey
So-Fluffy Mousse Bombe

(PAGE 131)

Mocha Sambuca Shooters

(PAGE 149)

Kelly's Island Chocolate
Coconut Rum Pie

(PAGE 154)

given the Pennsylvania Dutch (who are reputed to have conceived shoofly pie) something to talk about!

Although the biscuit/brownie pan for this recipe is an odd size, we found it in the kitchenware department at our Target store in Williamsburg.

For the Chocolate Shoofly Bites, I prefer a mild and sweet molasses such as Grandma's brand unsulfured. If you enjoy the assertive "bite" of blackstrap molasses, you may substitute an equal amount of it.

Use a small rubber spatula to facilitate removing all of the molasses and light corn syrup from the measuring cup.

The Chocolate Shoofly Bites will keep for several days stored in a tightly sealed plastic container in the refrigerator. To heighten the flavors, remove the bites from the refrigerator about 30 minutes before serving.

If you are a shoofly aficionado, you may prefer to cut larger portions of shoofly. Slightly warmed with a dollop or two of unsweetened whipped cream, they would be a gratifying eating experience, especially if accompanied by a tumbler filled with bourbon and a few cubes of ice. My, my!

Chocolate–Peanut Butter Birthday Fusion Brownie

PEANUT BUTTER–CREAM CHEESE FUSION

¾ cup creamy peanut butter

¼ pound cream cheese, cut into 1-ounce pieces

2 tablespoons granulated sugar

1 large egg yolk

⅓ cup sour cream

CHOCOLATE–PEANUT BUTTER BROWNIE

2 teaspoons unsalted butter, melted

¼ pound (1 stick) unsalted butter, cut into ½-ounce pieces

⅔ cup all-purpose flour

⅓ cup unsweetened cocoa powder

1 teaspoon baking powder

¼ teaspoon baking soda

¼ pound semisweet baking chocolate, coarsely chopped

¼ pound unsweetened baking chocolate, coarsely chopped

1½ cups granulated sugar

Whenever the subject of chocolate synergies arises, passionate disputation is certain. Some find the interaction between chocolate and raspberries to be unsurpassed. Others believe chocolate is lacking if some type of nut is not present, whether it's the crunch of an almond or the pleasing texture of peanut butter. For me, chocolate and peanut butter does it all.

MAKE THE PEANUT BUTTER–CREAM CHEESE FUSION Place the peanut butter, cream cheese, and sugar in the bowl of an electric mixer fitted with a paddle. Mix on low speed for 30 seconds; then increase the speed to medium and beat for 1 minute until combined. Use a rubber spatula to scrape down the sides of the bowl and the paddle. Add the egg yolk and beat on medium for 30 seconds. Scrape down the sides of the bowl and the paddle. Add the sour cream and beat on medium for 30 seconds until combined. Remove the bowl from the mixer and use a rubber spatula to finish mixing the ingredients until thoroughly combined. Set the mixture aside at room temperature until needed.

MAKE THE CHOCOLATE–PEANUT BUTTER BROWNIE Preheat the oven to 325°F.

Lightly coat the insides of a 9 × 13 × 2-inch nonstick rectangular baking pan with some of the melted butter. Line the bottom of the pan with parchment paper (or wax paper), then lightly coat the paper with more melted butter. Set aside.

In a sifter combine the flour, cocoa powder, baking powder, and baking soda. Sift onto a large piece of parchment paper (or wax paper) and set aside.

Melt the ¼ pound butter, the semisweet chocolate, and the unsweetened chocolate in the top half of a double boiler or in a medium glass bowl in a microwave oven (see pages 20–21); stir until smooth. Set aside.

Place the sugar and eggs in the bowl of an electric mixer fitted with a paddle (during the mixing process the sugar and egg mixture will create quite a bit of volume; depending on the size of the mixing bowl, you may want to use a pouring shield attachment or place a towel or plastic wrap over the top of the mixer and down the sides to the bowl to prevent the mixture from spewing out). Beat on medium-high speed for 4 minutes until slightly thickened and a pale ivory color. Add the chocolate and butter mixture and beat on medium for 30 seconds to combine. Operate the mixer on the lowest speed (stir) while gradually adding the dry ingredients; mix until incorporated, about 35 seconds. Scrape down the sides of the bowl. Add the peanut butter, sour cream, and vanilla extract and mix on low to combine, about 15 seconds. Now beat on medium for 20 seconds. Remove the bowl from the mixer and use a rubber spatula to finish mixing the batter until thoroughly combined.

Immediately pour about half (about 2¾ cups) of the brownie batter into the prepared pan and spread evenly to the edges of the pan. Pour the Peanut Butter–Cream Cheese Fusion mixture over the top of the brownie batter and use a spatula (an offset spatula works best) to spread evenly to the edges of the pan (don't worry, the brownie batter is dense enough to hold the weight of the fusion mixture). Now pour the remaining brownie batter over the fusion layer and again spread evenly to the edges of the pan.

Marbleize the brownie by dipping the flat blade of a dinner knife into the batter to the bottom of the pan, then lifting the blade of the knife out of the batter in a folding motion like the roll of a wave, repeating about 12 times throughout the batter in the pan. Smooth any air pockets on the surface of the batter with a spatula. Sprinkle the peanuts evenly over the batter. Bake on the center rack in the oven until a toothpick inserted into the center of the brownie comes out clean, 53 to 55 minutes. Remove the brownie from the oven and cool in the pan at room temperature for 30 minutes.

TO SERVE Invert the brownie onto a clean, dry cutting board, then turn back over. The brownie is ready to be served. You may want to present it whole with a candle or two, or cut into individual servings, deco-

5 large eggs
¾ cup creamy peanut butter
¼ cup sour cream
1½ teaspoons pure vanilla extract

PEANUT GARNISH
¼ cup unsalted dry-roasted peanuts, finely chopped

SERVES 12

rating each with a candle (let everyone share in the joy or pain). Use a serrated slicer to cut the brownie into twelve 3-inch squares. For a clean cut, heat the blade of the slicer under hot running water and wipe the blade dry before making each cut. Serve immediately, or store in a tightly sealed plastic container at room temperature.

$\mathcal{T}$HE CHEF'S TOUCH

The Chocolate–Peanut Butter Birthday Fusion Brownie will keep for 2 to 3 days at room temperature stored in a tightly sealed plastic container. For longer storage, 4 to 5 days, cover the squares with plastic wrap or store in a tightly sealed plastic container and refrigerate. Remove the brownies from the refrigerator 30 to 60 minutes before nibbling commences.

If you have attained voting age, why deprive yourself? Go for a mug of Hot Chocolate Buccaneer (page 160) with this brownie, and the nirvana created by the pairing will make you forget the furor over chads.

Slammin' Citrus Squares with White Chocolate–Lemon Balm Icing

Not long after commencing work as a pastry cook at The Trellis, Nicole Johnson decided to tantalize her co-workers with a batch of lemon squares. She uses fresh lemon juice rather than lemon extract. Ganache Hill test kitchen chef Brett Bailey thought Nicole's lemon squares would be terrific with a white chocolate icing, and he gave the squares an extra jolt of flavor by adding orange and lime zest, as well as fresh lemon balm. This collaboration between Nicole and Brett is a winner.

This bases-loaded grand slam sweetie should be along for the ride on your next outing, be that a baseball game or a picnic. The crunchy cookie crust that supports the tongue-twanging citrus center is a convenient vehicle for this handheld white chocolate–topped dessert.

MAKE THE 1-2-3 COOKIE CRUST Preheat the oven to 350°F. Lightly coat the inside of a 9 × 13 × 2-inch nonstick rectangular baking pan with some of the melted butter. Line the bottom of the pan with parchment paper (or wax paper), then lightly coat the paper with more melted butter. Set aside.

Place the ½ pound butter and the sugar in the bowl of an electric mixer fitted with a paddle. Mix on low speed for 1 minute; then beat on medium for 2 minutes until soft. Use a rubber spatula to scrape down the sides of the bowl. Continue beating on medium for an additional 2 minutes until softer. Add the flour and mix on the lowest speed (stir) to combine, about 1 minute. Scrape down the sides of the bowl and the paddle. Operate the mixer on low for about 20 seconds to finish combining the dough. Transfer the dough to the prepared pan. Wearing a pair of disposable vinyl (or latex) gloves, evenly press the dough into the bot-

1-2-3 COOKIE CRUST

2 teaspoons unsalted butter, melted

½ pound (2 sticks) unsalted butter, cut into ½-ounce pieces

⅓ cup granulated sugar

2 cups all-purpose flour, sifted

SUPER CITRUS CENTER

½ cup all-purpose flour

1 teaspoon baking powder

2¼ cups granulated sugar

6 large eggs

¾ cup fresh lemon juice

¼ cup minced orange zest

1 tablespoon minced lime zest

WHITE CHOCOLATE–LEMON BALM ICING

½ cup confectioners' sugar

8 ounces cream cheese, cut into 1-ounce pieces

¼ pound (1 stick) unsalted
   butter, cut into ½-ounce
   pieces
¼ pound white chocolate,
   coarsely chopped
1 tablespoon finely chopped
   fresh lemon balm leaves
   (for substitutes see
   page 91)

YIELDS TWENTY-FOUR 1¾- TO
2-INCH SQUARES

tom of the pan from the center to the edges in a uniform thickness (this is almost effortlessly accomplished as the dough is very malleable).

Bake on the center rack in the oven until the edges of the crust are lightly golden brown and have ever so slightly started to pull away from the sides of the pan, 20 to 21 minutes. Remove from the oven and set aside at room temperature while preparing the citrus center.

PREPARE THE SUPER CITRUS CENTER   Preheat the oven to 325°F.

In a sifter combine the flour and baking powder. Sift onto a large piece of parchment paper (or wax paper) and set aside.

Place the sugar and eggs in the bowl of an electric mixer fitted with a paddle. Beat on medium speed for 30 seconds until well combined. Add the lemon juice, orange zest, and lime zest and mix on low speed to combine, about 15 seconds. Add the dry ingredients and mix on the lowest speed (stir) until incorporated, about 30 seconds. Once the dry ingredients have been incorporated, stop the mixer and scrape down the sides of the bowl. Operate the mixer on low for 15 seconds to finish combining the ingredients. Pour the citrus mixture into the pan over the top of the baked cookie crust layer.

Bake on the center rack of the oven until golden brown and slightly firm to the touch, about 50 minutes (turn the pan 180 degrees about halfway through the baking time). Remove from the oven. Immediately use a small plastic knife to cut around all the edges of what is now the lemon bar to free it from the sides of the pan. Now, while the lemon bar is still hot (if it cools in the pan it will be very difficult to extricate), turn it out onto a parchment paper (or wax paper) covered baking sheet. Carefully peel the paper away from the crust. Refrigerate until cold, about 1 hour.

MAKE THE WHITE CHOCOLATE–LEMON BALM ICING   Sift the confectioners' sugar onto a large piece of parchment paper (or wax paper). Set aside.

Place the cream cheese and butter in the bowl of an electric mixer fitted with a paddle. Mix on low speed for 1 minute; then increase the speed to medium and beat for 2 minutes until soft. Use a rubber spatula to scrape down the sides of the bowl and the paddle. Beat on medium for

2 more minutes until very soft. Use a rubber spatula to scrape down the sides of the bowl and the paddle. Add the confectioners' sugar and mix on the lowest speed (stir) for 1 minute. Use a rubber spatula to scrape down the sides of the bowl.

Melt the white chocolate (see pages 20–21). While it is still warm (if it's not warm when added to the mixture, large lumps of chocolate may form) add it and 1 tablespoon fresh chopped lemon balm to the icing mixture. Now beat on medium for 1½ minutes until thoroughly combined and somewhat fluffy.

Remove the lemon bar from the refrigerator. Invert it (cookie crust layer down) onto a baking sheet. Use a cake spatula to evenly spread the lemon balm icing over the top and to the edges of the baked citrus center. Refrigerate for 1 hour before cutting.

TO SERVE Remove the lemon bar from the refrigerator and place on a clean, dry cutting board. Use a sharp knife to trim the edges of the lemon bar to create an approximately 8-inch-wide by 12-inch-long rectangle with smooth and even edges. Use a serrated slicer to cut the lemon bar into twenty-four 2-inch squares. For a clean cut, heat the blade of the slicer under lukewarm running water (don't get the blade too hot or it will melt the icing) and wipe the blade very dry before making each cut. Serve immediately, or store in a tightly sealed plastic container in the refrigerator.

THE CHEF'S TOUCH

You will need 5 to 6 lemons weighing about 4 ounces each to yield the ¾ cup fresh lemon juice; about 2½ oranges (8 ounces each) to yield the ¼ cup zest; and almost 1 whole lime (about 3 ounces) to yield the 1 tablespoon of zest.

If you are unable to find lemon balm and would like to use an herb, try lemon thyme in the same proportion; or for lemon flavor without an herb, substitute 1 tablespoon of finely minced lemon zest.

Slammin' Citrus Squares will keep for a couple of days at room temperature stored in a tightly sealed plastic container. For longer storage, 4 to 5 days, cover the squares with plastic wrap or store in a tightly sealed plastic container and refrigerate.

BLACK MAMBA COOKIES

1 pound semisweet baking
    chocolate, coarsely
    chopped

3 ounces unsweetened
    chocolate, coarsely
    chopped

¼ pound (1 stick) unsalted
    butter, cut into ½-ounce
    pieces

½ cup all-purpose flour

¼ cup unsweetened cocoa
    powder

¼ teaspoon baking powder

¼ teaspoon salt

4 large eggs

1 cup granulated sugar

2 tablespoons instant
    espresso powder

½ cup semisweet chocolate
    chips

¼ cup pecans, toasted
    (see page 23), and
    coarsely chopped

¼ cup walnuts, toasted and
    coarsely chopped

1 tablespoon pure vanilla
    extract

MAKES EIGHTEEN 3-INCH
COOKIES

Proffering these profoundly chocolate cookies leads to dangerous liaisons. Trellis pastry chef Kelly Bailey says this cookie batter has just enough flour to keep the chocolate and nuts together. Offer a black mamba to one you desire, and it may keep you together forever.

Preheat the oven to 325°F.

Melt the chopped semisweet chocolate, unsweetened chocolate, and butter in the top half of a double boiler or in a medium glass bowl in a microwave oven (see pages 20–21), and stir until smooth. Set aside.

In a sifter combine the flour, cocoa powder, baking powder, and salt. Sift onto a large piece of parchment paper (or wax paper) and set aside.

Place the eggs, sugar, and espresso powder in the bowl of an electric mixer fitted with a paddle. Beat on medium speed for 4 minutes until the mixture is thickened and slightly frothy. Add the chocolate and butter mixture and mix on medium to combine, about 1 minute. Use a rubber spatula to scrape down the sides of the bowl. Operate the mixer on low while gradually adding the dry ingredients; mix until incorporated, about 45 seconds. Scrape down the insides of the bowl. Add the chocolate chips, pecans, walnuts, and vanilla extract and mix on low to combine, about 10 seconds. Remove the bowl from the mixer and use a rubber spatula to finish mixing the ingredients until thoroughly combined. Note that a yummy batter-like consistency is achieved, rather than dough-like.

Using 3 heaping tablespoons (approximately 2½ ounces) or 1 heaping #20 ice cream scoop of the batter for each cookie; portion 6 cookies, evenly spaced, on each of 3 nonstick baking sheets. Place 1 baking sheet on the top rack and 1 baking sheet on the center rack of the oven and bake for 18 minutes, rotating the sheets from top to center halfway through the baking time (at that time also turn each sheet 180 degrees). The third baking sheet may be placed in another 325°F oven or held at room temperature and then baked after the first 2 sheets are removed from the oven. Remove the cookies from the oven and cool to room temperature on the baking sheets, about 15 minutes. Store the cooled cookies in a tightly sealed plastic container.

The Chef's Touch

Because of the batter-like rather than dough-like consistency of this cookie mixture you may prefer to prepare it in a large bowl, using a stiff wire whisk or even a rubber spatula rather than a standing electric mixer.

These cookies will stay fresh in a tightly sealed plastic container at room temperature for 2 to 3 days, or in the refrigerator for a week to 10 days (bring the cookies to room temperature before serving). For long-term storage, up to several weeks, the cookies may be frozen in a tightly sealed plastic container to prevent dehydration and freezer odors. Thaw the frozen cookies at room temperature before serving.

CHAMPAGNE FRITTERS WITH CHOCOLATE GRAPE SURPRISE AND SPARKLING CREAM

30 red seedless grapes,
stemmed, washed, and
thoroughly dried

4 ounces semisweet baking
chocolate, coarsely
chopped and melted
(see pages 20–21)

CHAMPAGNE FRITTERS

¾ cup all-purpose flour

1 tablespoon baking powder

1 tablespoon cornstarch

¼ teaspoon salt

3 tablespoons (1½ ounces)
tightly packed light
brown sugar

1 large egg white

3 ounces brut champagne or
dry American sparkling
wine, measured in a glass
cup measure

½ cup whole cashews,
toasted (see page 23) and
finely chopped

6 cups vegetable oil

Sweet or savory, fritters are deliciously easy to prepare and consume. My first experience with fritters and other deep-fried cakes was as a boy growing up in Rhode Island. My mom was quite expert in preparing a savory deep-fried cake that was fat and flavorful with quahog clams. Later on, while working at a local roadhouse restaurant during my high school years, a cook recently discharged from the Navy nicknamed "Frenchy" (which became my own sobriquet just a few years later when I was drafted into the Marine Corps) introduced me to apple fritters. Here's a dulcet confection so perfect for a New Year's Eve soirée . . . the crunchy hot exterior gives way to a cashew-laced interior that envelops a chocolate-coated grape. The lustrous whipped cream adds glamour. Ring in the new year with a tall flute of champagne.

PREPARE THE CHOCOLATE GRAPE SURPRISE   Place the grapes in a medium bowl.

Pour the semisweet chocolate over the grapes and use a rubber spatula to stir until each grape is completely coated with the melted chocolate.

Use a fork to transfer the grapes, one at a time, onto a parchment paper–lined (or wax paper–lined) baking sheet. Place the grapes in the freezer.

MAKE THE CHAMPAGNE FRITTERS   Preheat the oven to 325°F.

In a sifter combine the flour, baking powder, cornstarch, and salt. Sift onto a large piece of parchment paper (or wax paper) and set aside until needed.

In a medium bowl, use a rubber spatula to mix the tightly packed light brown sugar and egg white together until combined and all lumps of sugar have disappeared. Add the champagne and stir to combine. Add the cashews and stir to combine. Add the dry ingredients and stir until thoroughly combined. Set aside at room temperature while heating the vegetable oil.

Heat the vegetable oil in a deep fryer (or high-sided heavy-duty 4- to 5-quart saucepan) to a temperature of 350°F, about 15 minutes. Line a baking sheet with paper towels.

Remove the grapes from the freezer. Scoop about 1 tablespoon of the fritter batter into a #30 ice-cream scoop. Place a grape in the center of the batter in the scoop, then scoop a slightly heaping tablespoon of batter on top of the grape. Release the fritter into the hot oil. Fry until golden brown, about 1½ minutes. Repeat until all the fritters have been fried (once you get the knack of scooping, you should be able to fry 2 or 3 fritters at a time). Use tongs (or a slotted spoon) to remove the fritters from the oil and transfer to the baking sheet lined with paper towels. After all the fritters have been fried, place them on the baking sheet and put in the oven for 5 minutes to finish cooking. Refrigerate the remaining grapes. While the fritters are in the oven, prepare the Sparkling Cream.

PREPARE THE SPARKLING CREAM Place the heavy cream in the bowl of an electric mixer fitted with a balloon whip. Whisk on high speed until soft peaks form, 1½ to 2 minutes. Add the sugar and whisk to combine, about 10 seconds.

TO SERVE Spoon 3 to 4 heaping tablespoons of Sparkling Cream onto each serving plate. Place 2 hot Champagne Fritters on each portion of Sparkling Cream. Sift a light dusting of cocoa powder over the fritters and cream. Garnish each plate with the remaining grapes (4 per serving) and serve immediately.

THE CHEF'S TOUCH

Do you enjoy chocolate-covered raisins at the cinema? Hold on for an exponentially heightened pleasure with chocolate-covered grapes. Wash the stemmed grapes by placing them in a colander and spraying with lukewarm water. Allow the excess water to drain away, then dry the grapes thoroughly with paper towels.

SPARKLING CREAM

1 cup heavy cream

¼ cup turbinado sugar

COCOA DUSTING

2 tablespoons unsweetened cocoa powder

MAKES **10** FRITTERS

In order to produce moist fritters, measure the amount of champagne accurately by using a glass cup measure.

If a baking sheet will not fit into your freezer, place the chocolate-drenched grapes on a small platter or large dinner plate. Once frozen, the grapes may be stored in a tightly sealed plastic container in the freezer for several days.

Cashews are one of my favorite nuts—they taste voluptuous rather than unctuous. Other nuts such as pecans, hazelnuts, and another favorite, macadamias, could also be used for this recipe. Whichever you choose, be certain to toast the nuts (to accentuate the flavor), then cool them before finely chopping.

Processed to preserve some molasses flavor, turbinado sugar is readily available at the supermarket. Look for it under the brand name: Sugar in the Raw. The molasses gives the sugar a unique flavor and an appealing blond color.

If you don't intend to serve the fritters within a few minutes of removing them from the oven, you may lower the oven temperature to 200°F and keep the fritters warm, without drying them out, for up to 30 minutes before serving. If you need a bit more time before serving the fritters, hold them at room temperature for 2 to 3 hours after removing them from the oven, then reheat in a 325°F oven for 15 to 20 minutes until hot throughout.

For ease of service, whip the cream without the turbinado sugar 2 to 3 hours before serving (keep the whipped cream covered with plastic wrap in the refrigerator until needed). Use a whisk to combine the turbinado sugar with the whipped cream just before serving.

CHOCOLATE-CHUNK PINEAPPLE RUMMIES

Fancy the bite that yields a sumptuous morsel laden with rum-impregnated pineapple, toasty coconut, and ever so many chunks of chocolate. Not for kids, but you'll feel like one. Rummies are yummy!

Preheat the oven to 350°F.

Toast the coconut on a baking sheet in the oven until golden brown and crispy, about 3 minutes. Remove from the oven and set aside at room temperature.

Heat the pineapple pieces and ¼ cup of the rum in a small saucepan over medium heat. Bring to a boil; boil for 2 minutes until most of the rum has been absorbed by the pineapple pieces or has evaporated. Remove from the heat. Transfer the pineapple pieces to a dinner plate and spread evenly. Refrigerate.

In a sifter combine the flour, baking powder, and baking soda. Sift onto a large piece of parchment paper (or wax paper) and set aside until needed.

Place the butter and sugar in the bowl of an electric mixer fitted with a paddle. Mix on the lowest speed (stir) for 1 minute; then beat on medium for 2 minutes until soft. Use a rubber spatula to scrape down the sides of the bowl. Add the egg and egg yolk, one at a time, beating on medium for 30 seconds after each addition, and scraping down the sides of the bowl and the paddle once the egg and egg yolk have been incorporated. Now beat on medium for 30 more seconds. Operate the mixer on low while gradually adding half of the dry ingredients; mix until incorporated, about 45 seconds. Very gradually add the remaining ¼ cup dark rum and mix on low to incorporate, about 20 seconds. While continuing to operate the mixer on low, gradually add the remaining dry ingredients and mix for 30 seconds. Scrape down the sides of the bowl and the paddle. Add the coconut, the semisweet chocolate chunks, and the cooled,

¾ cup unsweetened dried grated coconut

1 cup ¼-inch-dice dried pineapple (about 4 dried pineapple rings)

½ cup Myers's dark rum

2 cups all-purpose flour

¼ teaspoon baking powder

¼ teaspoon baking soda

6 ounces unsalted butter, cut into ½-ounce pieces

¾ cup granulated sugar

1 large egg

1 large egg yolk

6 ounces semisweet chocolate chunks (page 98)

½ teaspoon pure coconut extract

MAKES EIGHTEEN 3-INCH COOKIES

rum-drenched pineapple. Mix on low for 10 seconds to incorporate. Scrape down the sides of the bowl. Add the coconut extract and mix on medium for 5 seconds. Remove the bowl from the mixer and use a rubber spatula to finish mixing the ingredients until thoroughly combined.

Using 2 heaping tablespoons (slightly more than 2 ounces), or a level #20 ice cream scoop of the rummie dough for each rummie, portion 6 rummies, evenly spaced, onto each of 3 nonstick baking sheets. Place 1 sheet on the top rack and 1 sheet on the center rack of the oven and bake for 20 minutes, rotating the sheets from top to center halfway through the baking time (at that time also turn each sheet 180 degrees). The third baking sheet may be placed in another 350°F oven or held at room temperature and then baked after the first 2 sheets are removed from the oven. Remove the rummies from the oven and cool to room temperature on the baking sheets, about 15 minutes. Store the cooled rummies in a tightly sealed plastic container.

$\mathcal{T}$HE CHEF'S TOUCH

Chocolate chunks made with real semisweet chocolate may be purchased at the supermarket. Baker's sells a 12-ounce package of chocolate chunks they describe as "Premium Chocolate for Indulgent Cookies." I myself cannot think of a more indulgent cookie than our rummie. Because of the rum injection, you may want to monitor the consumption, without causing disruption or interruption of munching.

You will find unsweetened dried grated coconut in the bulk food section at the supermarket, usually near the dried fruits (yes, dried pineapple rings) or nuts. Stay away from other types of packaged coconut for this recipe.

The Chocolate-Chunk Pineapple Rummies will stay fresh in a tightly sealed plastic container at room temperature for 4 to 5 days. I don't recommend refrigerating or freezing the rummies, as doing so adversely affects the texture and they just don't taste as mouth-watering.

If the flavor alliance of rum, pineapple, and coconut has you musing about a piña colada, palm trees, and white sandy beach gently sloping toward blue ocean, then I suggest pleasure awaits you in the rummie.

Dawn's Chocolate Cherry Whirly-Swirly Cookies

Dawn Bailey, Ganache Hill test kitchen chef Brett Bailey's sister-in-law, is the director of nursing at a world-renowned Cleveland, Ohio, hospital. Dawn loves to bake, especially cookies. In fact, she usually starts baking for the Christmas holidays right after Halloween. In the year 2000 she baked more than 300 dozen cookies. Dawn does a lot of research to come up with her own recipes; she is also organized about her cookie production, preparing and freezing the dough many weeks in advance, then baking for friends and family just days before the holidays. This one is a veritable vortex of cherries and chocolate, a soft-textured chocolate spiral that rolls alongside a crisp cherry swirl.

MAKE THE CHERRY COOKIE DOUGH Place the cherries in the mini-bowl of a food processor fitted with a metal blade. Process for 30 seconds until pureed (this should yield ½ cup pureed cherries). Set aside.

Place the butter and sugar in the bowl of an electric mixer fitted with a paddle. Mix on low speed for 1 minute, then on medium for 2 minutes until soft. Use a rubber spatula to scrape down the sides of the bowl and the paddle. Add the cherries, cherry extract, and red food color and mix on medium-low for 30 seconds, then beat on medium for 30 seconds. Scrape down the sides of the bowl. Operate the mixer on low while gradually adding the flour; mix until incorporated, about 45 seconds. Scrape down the sides of the bowl and the paddle. Now beat on medium until a dough is formed, about 30 seconds. Transfer the dough to a 12 × 20-inch piece of parchment paper (or wax paper). Use the palms of your hands to press the dough into an approximately 5 × 8 × 1-inch-thick rectangle. Place another 12 × 20-inch piece of paper over the dough. Use a rolling pin to roll the dough into an approximately 10 × 18 × ¼-inch-thick uniformly flat rectangle. (Unless you are a professional cookie dough roller, your rectangle will have rounded edges. Don't be concerned, these will be

CHERRY COOKIE DOUGH

5 ounces I.Q.F. (individually quick frozen) dark sweet cherries, thawed

6 ounces unsalted butter, cut into ½-ounce pieces

½ cup granulated sugar

1 tablespoon pure cherry extract

¼ teaspoon red food color

3 cups all-purpose flour, sifted onto a large piece of parchment paper (or wax paper)

CHOCOLATE COOKIE DOUGH

2 cups all-purpose flour

¼ cup unsweetened cocoa powder

½ pound (2 sticks) unsalted butter, cut into ½-ounce pieces

⅓ cup granulated sugar

4 ounces semisweet baking chocolate, coarsely chopped and melted (see pages 20–21)

1 tablespoon heavy cream
1 large egg white, lightly
   whisked

MAKES TWENTY-FOUR 3- TO
3½-INCH COOKIES

trimmed away.) Set aside at room temperature while preparing the Chocolate Cookie Dough.

PREPARE THE CHOCOLATE COOKIE DOUGH Preheat the oven to 325°F.

In a sifter combine the flour and cocoa powder. Sift onto a large piece of parchment paper (or wax paper) and set aside until needed.

Place the butter and sugar in the bowl of an electric mixer fitted with a paddle. Mix on low speed for 1 minute; then on medium for 2 minutes until soft. Use a rubber spatula to scrape down the sides of the bowl and the paddle. Add the semisweet chocolate, and mix on medium speed for 20 seconds. Thoroughly scrape down the sides of the bowl and the paddle. Operate the mixer on low while gradually adding the dry ingredients; mix until incorporated, about 1 minute. Scrape down the sides of the bowl. Add the heavy cream and mix on medium until combined and a dough is formed, about 45 seconds. Transfer the dough to a 12 × 20-inch piece of parchment paper (or wax paper). Use the palms of your hands to press the dough into an approximately 5 × 8 × ¾-inch-thick uniformly flat rectangle. Place another 12 × 20-inch piece of paper over the dough. Use a rolling pin to roll the dough into an approximately 10 × 18 × ¼-inch-thick rectangle.

Remove and discard the top pieces of paper from both the rectangles of dough. Lightly brush the top surfaces of the rectangles with the egg white (you will use about half the egg white; discard whatever remains). Invert the chocolate dough rectangle onto the cherry dough rectangle. (Now both pieces of dough will be sandwiched between 2 pieces of paper.) Use a rolling pin to lightly roll a few times over the paper on the chocolate dough (this will bond the doughs). Remove the paper from the top of the bonded dough. Starting with the narrow side (the 10-inch-wide side) nearest you, roll the bonded dough rectangle away from you, using the paper beneath to help lift the dough over onto itself (this will create an interior spiral of the two doughs). Continue to roll the dough to the opposite end, making a tight roll. Now wrap the paper around the dough (from this point I will refer to the dough as a roll). Wrap the roll with plastic wrap and refrigerate until very firm, about 2 hours.

Remove the roll from the refrigerator and place on a clean, dry cutting board. Remove and discard the paper and the plastic wrap. Cut 1 inch off each end of the roll and discard (each end will now be flat). Cut the roll into 24 individual ⅜-inch-thick slices. Divide the slices among 3 nonstick baking sheets, 8 evenly spaced slices per sheet.

Place 1 baking sheet on the top rack and 1 baking sheet on the center rack of the oven and bake for 19 to 20 minutes, rotating the sheets from top to center halfway through the baking time (at that time also turn each sheet 180 degrees). The third baking sheet may be placed in another 325°F oven or held at room temperature and then baked after the first 2 sheets are removed from the oven. Remove the cookies from the oven and cool to room temperature on the baking sheets, about 20 minutes. Store the cooled cookies in a tightly sealed plastic container.

THE CHEF'S TOUCH

Find cherry extract near the vanilla extract on the spice aisle at your supermarket.

Dawn's Chocolate Cherry Whirly-Swirly Cookies will keep for 2 to 3 days at room temperature if stored in a tightly sealed plastic container. For long-term storage, up to several weeks, the cookies may be frozen. Freeze in a tightly sealed plastic container to prevent dehydration and permeation by freezer odors.

WHITE CHOCOLATE–
BUTTERSCOTCH COOKIES

8 ounces white chocolate,
coarsely chopped

2 ounces unsalted butter, cut
into ½-ounce pieces

2 cups all-purpose flour

¼ teaspoon baking powder

¼ teaspoon baking soda

¼ teaspoon salt

½ cup granulated sugar

3 large eggs

½ teaspoon pure vanilla
extract

¾ cup butterscotch chips

½ cup skinned hazelnuts,
toasted (see page 23) and
cut in half

MAKES EIGHTEEN 3½- TO
4-INCH COOKIES

Feeling giddy about white chocolate? Imagine the elation of a white chocolate cookie chock-full of butterscotch chips and toasted hazelnuts. With this recipe, you'll find yourself on cloud nine.

Preheat the oven to 325°F.

Melt the white chocolate in the top half of a double boiler, or in a medium bowl in a microwave oven (see pages 20–21), and stir until smooth. Set aside.

Place the butter in a small glass bowl in a microwave oven set at medium power for 45 seconds. Remove from the microwave oven and use a rubber spatula to stir the butter until its melted, smooth, and creamy. Set aside.

In a sifter combine the flour, baking powder, baking soda, and salt. Sift onto a large piece of parchment paper (or wax paper) and set aside.

Place the sugar and eggs in the bowl of an electric mixer fitted with a paddle. Beat on medium-high speed for 3 minutes until light in color and thickened. Add the white chocolate and mix on medium for 1 minute. Add the butter and mix on medium to combine, about 15 seconds. Operate the mixer on low while gradually adding the dry ingredients. Once they have been incorporated, 50 to 60 seconds, stop the mixer and scrape down the sides of the bowl. Add the vanilla extract and mix on low speed to combine, about 10 seconds. Add the butterscotch chips and the hazelnut halves and mix on low to combine, about 10 seconds. Remove the bowl from the mixer and use a rubber spatula to finish mixing the batter until thoroughly combined.

Using 2 heaping tablespoons (about 2 ounces), or a level #20 ice cream scoop of the rather sticky batter (because of the stickiness of the batter, this cookie is a bit difficult to portion, but not to worry—the worst-case scenario is one or two portions of cookie batter more or less) for each cookie, portion 6 cookies, evenly spaced, onto each of 3 non-stick baking sheets. Place 1 baking sheet on the top rack and 1 baking sheet on the center rack of the oven and bake for 13 to 14 minutes, rotating the sheets from top to center halfway through the baking time (at that time also turn each sheet 180 degrees). The third baking sheet may be placed in another 325°F oven or held at room temperature and then baked after the first 2 sheets are removed from the oven. Remove the cookies from the oven and cool to room temperature on the baking sheets, about 15 minutes. Store the cooled cookies in a tightly sealed plastic container.

𝒯HE CHEF'S TOUCH

The microwave is my preferred method for melting butter when an emulsified, creamy, and viscous liquid is desired. Melting the butter over direct heat usually causes separation of milk fat, water, and milk solids. The sauce-like consistency of the butter melted by the microwave method contributes greatly to the soft, almost cake-like texture of this cookie. If too much time elapses between melting and using the butter in the cookie batter, the butter may solidify. If the butter becomes too thick to pour, put it back in the microwave for a few seconds, or warm it over slightly hot water (not simmering) for a few moments, then stir until smooth and cohesive.

White Chocolate–Butterscotch Cookies will stay fresh in a tightly sealed plastic container at room temperature for 2 to 3 days, or in the refrigerator for a week to 10 days (bring the cookies to room temperature before consuming). For long-term storage, up to several weeks, the cookies may be frozen in a tightly sealed plastic container to prevent dehydration and permeation by freezer odors. Thaw the frozen cookies at room temperature before serving.

FROZEN DESSERTS

Brrr. . . . these impossibly decadent desserts are so
luscious it's hard to believe they're frozen. But they'll
remove the chill from any celebration whether you're
feeling patriotic with the Red, White, and Blue Berry
Ice Cream, or want to be all dressed up with a
Caramel Orange–Chocolate Orange Masquerade
Ice Cream Terrine.

CARAMEL ORANGE– CHOCOLATE ORANGE MASQUERADE ICE CREAM TERRINE

If you're looking for a real, honest, neighborhood restaurant full of faithful Parisian diners, this is it." As this was what I wanted for my first meal in a restaurant in France on July 1, 1985, I followed this advice from Patricia Wells in her *Food Lover's Guide to Paris* and headed for the bistro A Sousceyrac. All of my expectations of French food at the source were exceeded and most especially so with dessert: a large slab of the most sublime chocolate ice cream studded with nuts and presented with warm dark chocolate sauce. We have served countless different ice cream terrines at The Trellis ever since, and pastry chef Kelly Bailey's creation is one of my favorites.

MAKE THE CARAMEL ORANGE ICE CREAM   Line a medium 8³/₈ × 4³/₈ × 2³/₈-inch nonstick loaf pan with a 12 × 18-inch piece of plastic wrap (the overhanging plastic wrap will be used to remove the frozen ice cream terrine from the pan). Set aside.

Place ¹/₂ cup of the sugar and the lemon juice in a medium saucepan. Stir with a long-handled stainless steel kitchen spoon to combine. (The sugar will resemble moist sand.)

Caramelize the sugar for about 5 minutes over medium-high heat, stirring constantly with the spoon to break up any lumps. The sugar will first turn clear as it liquefies, then light brown as it caramelizes. Remove the saucepan from the heat. Gradually add the heavy cream to the bubbling hot sugar, whisking vigorously with a 12-inch-long balloon whisk until the mixture stops bubbling. (Adding the cream to the sugar creates very hot steam; be careful to avoid a steam burn on your whisking hand.)

CARAMEL ORANGE ICE CREAM

¾ cup granulated sugar

½ teaspoon fresh lemon juice

1½ cups heavy cream

1½ cups half-and-half

¼ cup fresh orange juice

2 tablespoons minced orange zest

3 large egg yolks

CHOCOLATE ORANGE MASQUERADE

12 ounces semisweet baking chocolate, coarsely chopped

5 ounces unsalted butter, cut into ½-ounce pieces

¼ cup heavy cream

¼ cup fine julienne of orange zest

SERVES **8**

Add the half-and-half, orange juice, and orange zest and stir to incorporate. Return to the heat and bring to a boil over medium-high heat (placing the long-handled kitchen spoon in the cream mixture to dissolve the hardened caramel on the spoon is effective).

While the cream mixture is heating, place the egg yolks and the remaining ¼ cup sugar in the bowl of an electric mixer fitted with a paddle. Beat on medium-high speed for 2 minutes until thoroughly combined; then use a rubber spatula to scrape down the sides of the bowl and the paddle. Beat on medium-high for an additional 2 minutes until slightly thickened and pale yellow. If at this point the cream mixture has not yet started to boil, adjust the mixer speed to low and continue to mix until it does boil; otherwise lumps may form when the boiling cream mixture is added. Gradually pour the boiling cream mixture into the egg yolk and sugar mixture and mix on low to combine, about 30 seconds. (To avoid splattering the boiling cream mixture, use a pouring shield attachment, or place a towel or plastic wrap over the top of the mixer and down the sides of the bowl.)

Return the combined mixture to the saucepan, using a rubber spatula to facilitate transferring all of the mixture, then heat over medium heat, stirring constantly. Bring to a temperature of 185°F, 2½ to 3 minutes. Use an instant-read thermometer for an accurate temperature reading of the mixture. Remove from the heat and transfer to a large stainless steel bowl. Cool in an ice water bath to a temperature of 40° to 45°F. Freeze in an ice cream machine, following the manufacturer's instructions. Transfer the semifrozen ice cream to the plastic wrap–lined loaf pan. Spread the ice cream evenly with a spatula (a small offset spatula works best). Cover the ice cream in the pan with plastic wrap, then place in the freezer for several hours until the ice cream is hard.

MAKE THE CHOCOLATE ORANGE MASQUERADE Melt the semisweet chocolate, butter, and heavy cream in the top half of a double boiler or in a large glass bowl in a microwave oven (see pages 20-21), and stir until smooth. Reserve ¾ cup of the melted chocolate; add the julienne of orange zest to the remaining melted chocolate and stir to incorporate.

Remove the hardened ice cream terrine from the freezer. Remove the plastic wrap on the top of the ice cream and discard. Pour the reserved ¾ cup of melted chocolate over the top of the ice cream in the pan and use a small offset spatula to spread the chocolate evenly to the edges. Return to the freezer for 20 minutes until the chocolate is hard.

Place a cooling rack on a baking sheet with sides. Remove the ice cream terrine from the freezer. Use the overhanging edges of the plastic wrap to pull the ice cream out of the pan. Invert the ice cream terrine, chocolate side down, onto the cooling rack. Remove and discard the plastic wrap. Pour the remaining melted chocolate and orange zest julienne over the ice cream terrine, allowing the chocolate to flow over the top and sides of the terrine. Use a utility turner (wide spatula) to transfer the ice cream terrine to a clean baking sheet. Place in the freezer for at least 30 minutes before cutting.

TO SERVE   Use a serrated slicer to cut about ⅛ inch of the ends from the terrine; cut the terrine into 8 slices about 1 inch thick (wipe the blade clean before cutting each slice). Serve immediately.

ℱHE CHEF'S TOUCH

Brett purchased the odd-size medium 8⅜ × 4⅛ × 2⅜-inch nonstick loaf pan at the supermarket.

For this recipe, you will need one 8-ounce orange to yield ¼ cup orange juice and 2 tablespoons of zest, and an additional two 8-ounce oranges to yield ¼ cup fine julienne of zest.

The Caramel Orange–Chocolate Orange Masquerade Ice Cream Terrine will keep for several days in the freezer when stored in a tightly sealed plastic container.

Although this ice cream terrine needs no embellishment, I am not the kind of guy who leaves well enough alone. Try heating orange segments in Grand Marnier. Once the segments are ever so slightly warmed and imbued with the liqueur, spoon them with their boozy liquid onto each serving plate alongside each slice of ice cream terrine.

Chocolate-Banana-Rum-Raisin Ice Cream Cakes with Rum and Almond Twinkle

BANANA RUM ICE CREAM

½ cup tightly packed (4
    ounces) light brown sugar

2 ounces unsalted butter, cut
    into ½-ounce pieces

1½ pounds ripe medium
    bananas, unpeeled

¾ cup Myers's dark rum plus
    1 tablespoon

2 cups heavy cream

1 cup half-and-half

4 large egg yolks

¼ cup granulated sugar

CHOCOLATE-RUM-RAISIN CAKES

2 teaspoons unsalted butter,
    melted

2 ounces unsalted butter, cut
    into ½-ounce pieces

½ cup cake flour

⅛ teaspoon baking powder

4 ounces semisweet baking
    chocolate, coarsely
    chopped

½ cup raisins

¼ cup Myers's dark rum

With just shy of a pint of dark rum, these cakes are not for the abstemious. Creamy rum-infused caramelized banana ice cream holds court on a deeply dark rum-flavored chocolate cake. Top that with rum-coated slivers of almonds. If you're seeking a many-splendored thing, I recommend serving warm caramelized bananas (prepare as described in the ice cream recipe) along with the ice cream cakes. Sweet dreams are made of such things. Any suggestions on how to dispatch the remaining shot of rum?

PREPARE THE BANANA RUM ICE CREAM   Heat the brown sugar and butter in a medium nonstick sauté pan over medium heat. When the mixture is hot, stir to dissolve the sugar. Bring to a boil. Peel the bananas and cut each one in quarters lengthwise, then cut each quarter into ½-inch pieces. Immediately add the bananas to the boiling sugar and butter mixture. Cook the bananas for 1 minute while stirring constantly with a rubber spatula. Add ¼ cup of the rum and stir to incorporate. Cook the bananas for an additional 2 minutes, stirring occasionally. Remove from the heat, then strain the bananas, reserving the liquid. Transfer the bananas to a baking sheet with sides and spread evenly, then set aside. Return the reserved liquid to the saucepan with ½ cup of the rum and bring to a boil over medium heat. Boil until the mixture has the viscosity of a thick syrup and has reduced to ½ cup, about 4 minutes. Pour the syrup over the bananas to coat (if you can resist the allure of tasting a spoonful of the caramelized bananas, you are a much less indulgent person than I am), then refrigerate.

Heat the heavy cream and half-and-half in a medium saucepan over medium high heat. Bring to a boil.

While the cream mixture is coming to a boil place the egg yolks and granulated sugar in the bowl of an electric mixer fitted with a paddle. Beat on high speed for 2 minutes until thoroughly combined, then use a rubber spatula to scrape down the sides of the bowl. Beat on high for an additional 2 minutes until slightly thickened and pale yellow. If at this point the cream mixture has not yet started to boil, adjust the mixer speed to low and continue to mix until it does boil; otherwise, lumps may form when the boiling cream mixture is added.

Gradually pour the boiling cream mixture into the egg yolks and sugar and mix on medium-low to combine, about 1 minute. (To avoid splattering the cream mixture, use a pouring shield attachment, or place a towel or plastic wrap over the top of the mixer and down the sides to the bowl.)

Return the combined mixture to the saucepan (use a rubber spatula to facilitate transferring all of the mixture); heat over medium heat, stirring constantly. Bring to a temperature of 185°F, about 3 minutes. Use an instant-read thermometer for an accurate temperature reading of the mixture. Remove from the heat and transfer to a large stainless steel bowl. Cool in an ice water bath to a temperature of 40° to 45°F.

When the mixture is cold, freeze in an ice cream machine, following the manufacturer's instructions. Transfer the semifrozen ice cream to a 2-quart plastic container. Add the chilled banana pieces and the remaining 1 tablespoon of rum; use a rubber spatula to fold the bananas and rum into the ice cream. Cover the container, then place in the freezer while making the individual cakes.

MAKE THE CHOCOLATE-RUM-RAISIN CAKES Preheat the oven to 325°F.

Assemble six 4 × 1½-inch nonstick springform pans with the bottom insert turned over (the lip of the insert facing down). Lightly coat the insides of the springform pans using the melted butter. Set aside.

In a sifter combine the cake flour and baking powder. Sift onto a large piece of parchment paper (or wax paper), and set aside.

Melt the semisweet chocolate and the 2 ounces butter in the top half of a double boiler or in a small glass bowl in the microwave oven (see pages 20–21), and stir until smooth. Set aside.

Heat the raisins with the rum in a small nonstick sauté pan over

1 large egg
1 large egg yolk
2 tablespoons granulated sugar

RUM AND ALMOND TWINKLE
¾ cup Myers's dark rum
¼ cup granulated sugar
1¼ cups (6 ounces) slivered almonds, toasted (see page 23)

MAKES **6** INDIVIDUAL CAKES

medium heat. Bring to a boil. Boil the mixture until the raisins have absorbed almost all of the rum, about 1½ minutes. Set aside.

Place the egg, egg yolk, and sugar in the bowl of an electric mixer fitted with a paddle. Beat on high speed for 5 minutes, until slightly thickened and pale yellow. Use a rubber spatula to scrape down the sides of the bowl and paddle. Add the chocolate and butter mixture and mix on medium to combine, about 20 seconds. Operate the mixer on low while gradually adding the dry ingredients; mix until incorporated, about 45 seconds. Remove the bowl from the mixer, add the raisins, and use a rubber spatula to finish mixing the ingredients until thoroughly combined. Portion a level #20 ice cream scoop (2 ounces) of the batter into each prepared pan and spread evenly. At this point you probably will be tempted to taste the darkly delicious looking batter—don't, unless you would like to meet Sal (salmonella, that is). Place the pans on a baking sheet, then place on the center rack of the oven and bake until a toothpick inserted in the center of a cake comes out clean, 11 to 12 minutes (turn the sheet 180 degrees after 6 minutes). Remove the cakes from the oven and cool in the pans at room temperature for 10 minutes. Refrigerate the cakes (in the pans) for at least 30 minutes.

ASSEMBLE THE ICE CREAM CAKES   Remove the cakes from the refrigerator and the ice cream from the freezer. Divide the ice cream equally among the pans, and spread the ice cream evenly. Use a small offset spatula to smooth the ice cream level with the top edge of each pan. (If the ice cream is too hard to spread evenly, allow it to soften at room temperature for about 10 minutes.) Cover the top of each pan tightly with plastic wrap and freeze for at least 12 hours until the ice cream is solid to the touch.

MAKE THE RUM AND ALMOND TWINKLE   While the cakes are in the freezer make the Rum and Almond Twinkle.

Preheat the oven to 300°F.

Heat the rum and sugar in a medium nonstick saute pan over medium heat. When warm, stir to dissolve the sugar. Bring to a boil. When the mixture begins to boil, add the almonds. Boil the rum and almonds until the rum has almost completely evaporated, about 7 minutes. Transfer the almonds to a baking sheet with sides and spread evenly toward the sides with a rubber spatula. Bake in the oven until the almonds are a dark golden brown color, 16 to 17 minutes. Cool the almonds at room temperature. When the nuts are cool, use your hands to break up any nuts that have clustered together (the idea is to have the nut slivers as individual as possible). Store the nuts at air-conditioned room temperature (68° to 78°F).

TO SERVE   Remove the cakes from the freezer. Discard the plastic wrap. Let the cakes stand at room temperature for 5 minutes. Sprinkle about ⅓ cup (a bit more than 1 ounce) of the Twinkle over the ice cream on each cake. Use your hands to press the Twinkle into place on the ice cream. Release the cakes from the springform pans. If the cakes do not release, one at a time wrap a damp, hot towel around the sides of a pan (the towel should be large enough to completely wrap around and cover the sides of the pan). Hold the towel tightly around the pan for 30 to 45 seconds, then release the cake from the sides of the pan. Use a metal spatula to remove the cakes from the bottom insert of the pans. Serve immediately.

𝒯HE CHEF'S TOUCH

The required 1½ pounds of unpeeled bananas will yield 12 to 14 ounces of peeled fruit. For the optimum banana flavor in the ice cream, don't use over- or under-ripe bananas. Pick bananas that are predominantly yellow with few if any green or brown spots. These bananas will have just the firm texture and subtlety of flavor necessary.

The uniquely sized 4 × 1½-inch nonstick springform pans used in this recipe are available from Wilton Enterprises (see Online Sources, page 161). Wilton calls the pans Singles!, I call them fun. Even though the pans are manufactured to last for many years, they are inexpensive.

Turning over the bottom inserts of the springform pans (with the lip of the bottom inserts facing down) before assembling the pans will make it easier to remove the finished desserts from the bottoms of the pans.

After assembly, you may keep the Chocolate-Banana-Rum-Raisin Ice Cream Cakes in the freezer for several days. Of course you may serve one cake or all six at a time. To avoid permeating the cakes with freezer odors, keep tightly covered with plastic wrap until ready to serve.

These cakes may be prepared over 3 days.

Day 1: Make and freeze the Banana Rum Ice Cream. Bake the individual Chocolate-Rum-Raisin Cakes. Cool the cakes, then refrigerate.

DAY 2: Remove the cakes from the refrigerator and the ice cream from the freezer; assemble the cakes as directed in the recipe. If the ice cream is too hard to spread, soften (but don't thaw) it in the refrigerator for 45 to 60 minutes before spreading. Cover each with plastic wrap and place in the freezer.

DAY 3: Prepare the Rum and Almond Twinkle. Once the Twinkle has cooled to room temperature, finish and serve the cakes as described in the recipe.

CHOCOLATE COOKIE CRUMBLE SPIKED BERRY ICE CREAM CAKE

This frozen confection, which dares to pair cranberries along with chocolate, will be much appreciated as the culmination of most Thanksgiving feasts. With the myriad last-minute cooking that needs to be done when families of all sizes gather, it's nice to know that dessert can be prepared several days in advance. By using dried cranberries and frozen raspberries, you can make this dessert any month of the year; so although it's nice to have it in the freezer for that special Thursday in November, you can serve it any Thursday.

MAKE THE CHOCOLATE COOKIE CRUMBLE CRUST Preheat the oven to 325°F.

Melt the semisweet chocolate and unsweetened chocolate in the top half of a double boiler or in a small glass bowl in the microwave oven (see pages 20–21) and stir until smooth. Set aside.

In a sifter combine the flour, baking soda, and salt. Sift onto a large piece of parchment paper (or wax paper) and set aside until needed.

Place the ¼ pound butter, the granulated sugar, and the brown sugar in the bowl of an electric mixer fitted with a paddle. Mix on low speed for 1 minute, then beat on medium for 3 minutes until soft and thoroughly combined. Use a rubber spatula to scrape down the sides of the bowl. Add the eggs, one at a time, beating on medium for 30 seconds after each addition, and scraping down the sides of the bowl once the eggs have been incorporated. Beat on medium speed until very soft, about 2 minutes. Add the melted chocolate and mix on medium for 15 seconds, then scrape down the sides of the bowl. Operate the mixer on low while gradually adding the dry ingredients; mix until incorporated, about 30 seconds. Add the vanilla extract and mix on medium to combine, about 10 seconds. Remove the bowl from the mixer and use a rubber spatula to finish mixing the ingredients until thoroughly combined.

CHOCOLATE COOKIE CRUMBLE CRUST

3 ounces semisweet baking chocolate, coarsely chopped

2 ounces unsweetened baking chocolate, coarsely chopped

¾ cup all-purpose flour

½ teaspoon baking soda

¼ teaspoon salt

¼ pound (1 stick) unsalted butter, cut into ½-ounce pieces

½ cup granulated sugar

½ cup (4 ounces) tightly packed light brown sugar

2 large eggs

1½ teaspoons pure vanilla extract

3 tablespoons unsalted butter, melted

SPIKED BERRY ICE CREAM

1 cup dried cranberries

¾ cup brandy plus 1 tablespoon

One 10-ounce package
frozen whole red
raspberries, thawed
1¾ cups heavy cream
½ cup granulated sugar
2 large egg yolks

BRANDY GANACHE
4 ounces semisweet baking
chocolate, coarsely
chopped
½ cup heavy cream
2 tablespoons brandy

SERVES 8 TO 10

Using 3 slightly heaping tablespoons (approximately 2 ounces) or 1 heaping #20 ice cream scoop of the batter, portion 6 cookies, evenly spaced, onto each of 2 nonstick baking sheets. Place the baking sheets on the top and center racks of the oven and bake for 35 minutes, rotating the sheets from top to center halfway through the baking time (at that time also turn each sheet 180 degrees). Remove the cookies from the oven and cool to room temperature on the baking sheets, about 10 minutes. Don't be dismayed by the appearance of the cookies: collapsed and wrinkled. Despite their looks they are perfect for the cookie crust, crisp on the outside and moist in the center. Refrigerate for 15 minutes.

Break the chilled cookies into quarters, then place the quarters in a food processor fitted with a metal blade (depending on the size of your food processor, you may have to do this in two batches). Pulse the cookies until very fine, about 45 seconds. Add the 3 tablespoons melted butter and pulse for 15 seconds. Transfer half the amount (2¼ cups) of crumbs to the bottom of a 9 × 1¾-inch springform pan. Spread the crumbs evenly over the bottom of the pan, then press firmly until smooth and even (wearing a pair of disposable vinyl or latex gloves makes this job much less messy). Firmly press the remaining crumbs into the sides of the pan as evenly and uniformly as possible. Place on a baking sheet (this makes removing the pan from the oven much easier) on the center rack of the oven and bake for 12 minutes. Remove from the oven and cool at room temperature.

MAKE THE SPIKED BERRY ICE CREAM Heat the cranberries and the ¾ cup brandy in a medium saucepan over medium-high heat. Bring to a boil, then adjust heat and simmer for 15 minutes, stirring occasionally, until all the liquid has evaporated. Transfer the berries to a small bowl, let cool, and refrigerate.

Puree the raspberries in the bowl of a food processor fitted with a metal blade for 30 seconds.

Heat the heavy cream and ¼ cup of the sugar in a medium saucepan over medium high-heat. When hot, stir to dissolve the sugar. Bring to a boil.

While the cream mixture is heating, place the egg yolks and the remaining ¼ cup sugar in the bowl of an electric mixer fitted with a paddle. Beat on high speed for 2 minutes, until thoroughly combined; then use a rubber spatula to scrape down the sides of the bowl and the paddle. Beat on high for an additional 2 minutes until slightly thickened and pale yellow. If at this point the cream mixture has not yet started to boil, adjust the mixer speed to low and continue to mix until it does boil; otherwise, lumps may form when the boiling cream mixture is added. Gradually pour the boiling cream mixture into the egg yolk and sugar mixture and mix on low to combine, about 1 minute (to avoid splattering the boiling cream mixture, use a pouring shield attachment, or place a towel or plastic wrap over the top of the mixer and down the sides to the bowl). Return the combined mixture to the saucepan, using a rubber spatula to facilitate transferring all of the mixture; heat over medium heat, stirring constantly. Bring to a temperature of 185°F, 2 to 3 minutes. Use an instant-read thermometer for an accurate temperature reading of the mixture. Remove from the heat and transfer to a large stainless steel bowl. Add the raspberries, the cranberries, and the remaining 1 tablespoon brandy and stir to combine. Cool in an ice water bath to a temperature of 40° to 45°F.

When the mixture is cold, freeze in an ice cream machine, following the manufacturer's instructions. Transfer the semifrozen ice cream into the chocolate cookie crumble shell, and use a rubber spatula to spread the ice cream into a smooth, even surface. Cover the top of the ice cream with plastic wrap (this is to protect the ice cream from acquiring freezer odors). Freeze for at least 12 hours or overnight until the ice cream is solid to the touch.

AFTER 12 HOURS, PREPARE THE BRANDY GANACHE   Place the chopped semisweet chocolate in a medium bowl.

Heat the heavy cream and brandy in a medium saucepan over medium-high heat. Bring to a boil. Pour the boiling cream over the chocolate. Stir with a whisk until smooth, then place the bowl in the refrigerator for 5 minutes to cool the ganache so that it will not melt the ice cream in the next step.

Remove the ice cream cake from the freezer, then carefully remove and discard the plastic wrap. Pour the ganache (as long as you did not refrigerate for more than 5 minutes, the ganache should be pourable) on top of the ice cream layer. Use a small offset spatula (or a rubber spatula) to spread the ganache evenly over the surface of the ice cream. Place the cake in the freezer for at least an hour before serving.

TO SERVE Remove the cake from the freezer. Heat the blade of a serrated slicer under hot running water and wipe the blade dry before making each slice. Serve immediately and prepare yourself for the kudos, because this may be the most amazing ice cream cake your guests have ever enjoyed.

*T*HE CHEF'S TOUCH

After assembly, you may keep the cake in the freezer for several days. To avoid permeating the cake with freezer odors, place the cake in a large, tightly sealed plastic container.

This cake may be prepared over 3 days.

DAY 1: Bake the cookies for the Chocolate Cookie Crumble Crust. Form the crust in the springform pan. Bake as directed. Once baked, cool to room temperature, then refrigerate until the next day.

DAY 2: Make the ice cream. Spread the ice cream in the baked crust as directed in the recipe. Cover with plastic wrap and place in the freezer.

DAY 3: Make the ganache, then spread it over the ice cream and return to the freezer for 1 hour before cutting and serving.

CHOCOLATE GRASSHOPPER ICE CREAM SANDWICH

You won't find an ice cream sandwich like our Grasshopper concoction at the corner convenience store, and for good reason. This refined adaptation of a southern favorite, Grasshopper Pie, would seem out of place sharing freezer space with the more ordinary standards youngsters devour on one of those sultry midsummer days. The mint is fresh, the green crème de menthe is sassy, and the chocolate cake that wedges the ice cream is sublime enough to handle them both.

MAKE THE CHOCOLATE GRASSHOPPER CAKE   Preheat the oven to 325°F. Lightly coat the insides of two 10¾ × 7 × 1½-inch nonstick biscuit/brownie pans with some of the melted butter. Line the bottoms of the pans with parchment paper (or wax paper), then lightly coat the paper with more melted butter. Set aside.

In a sifter combine the flour, cocoa powder, baking powder, and salt. Sift onto a large piece of parchment paper (or wax paper) and set aside.

Melt the 3 ounces butter, semisweet chocolate, and unsweetened chocolate in the top half of a double boiler, or in a glass bowl in a microwave oven (see pages 20–21) and stir until smooth.

Place the eggs and sugar in the bowl of an electric mixer fitted with a paddle. Beat on high speed for 3 minutes, until slightly thickened and light in color. (To avoid splattering the egg and sugar mixture, use a pouring shield attachment, or place a towel or plastic wrap over the top of the mixer and down the sides to the bowl.) Add the chocolate and butter mixture and beat on medium for 15 seconds to combine, then use a rubber spatula to scrape down the sides of the bowl. Operate the mixer on low while gradually adding the dry ingredients; mix until incorporated, about 30 seconds. Scrape down the sides of the bowl. Add the sour cream and mint and beat on medium for 20 seconds to combine. Remove the bowl from the mixer and use a rubber spatula to finish mix-

CHOCOLATE GRASSHOPPER CAKE

2 teaspoons unsalted butter, melted

3 ounces unsalted butter cut into ½-ounce pieces

½ cup all-purpose flour

¼ cup unsweetened cocoa powder

¼ teaspoon baking powder

¼ teaspoon salt

2 ounces semisweet baking chocolate, coarsely chopped

1 ounce unsweetened baking chocolate, coarsely chopped

3 large eggs

½ cup granulated sugar

¼ cup sour cream

1 teaspoon chopped fresh mint

CRÈME DE MENTHE
ICE CREAM

1 cup heavy cream

1 cup half-and-half

½ cup granulated sugar

2 tablespoons chopped fresh
    mint

3 large egg yolks

1 tablespoon green crème de
    menthe

½ cup semisweet chocolate
    mini-morsels

MAKES **12** SANDWICHES

ing the ingredients until thoroughly combined (this batter is exception-ally fragrant, but don't taste it—ingesting raw egg yolks is not salutary).

Immediately divide the cake batter into the prepared pans (about 1½ cups in each pan) and spread as evenly as possible. I suggest using an offset spatula to do the spreading. The batter is so dense that it will bake unevenly if not spread evenly over the entire surface of the pan bottoms. Bake on the center rack of the oven until a toothpick inserted into the centers of the cake layers comes out clean, about 15 minutes (rotate the position of the pans from left to right halfway through the baking time and turn each 180 degrees). Remove the cake layers from the oven and cool in the pans for 5 minutes at room temperature. Invert the cake layers onto baking sheets lined with parchment paper (or wax paper). Carefully peel the paper away from the bottoms of the cake layers. Refrigerate the cake layers while making the ice cream.

MAKE THE CRÈME DE MENTHE ICE CREAM   Heat the heavy cream, half-and-half, ¼ cup of the sugar, and mint in a medium saucepan over medium-high heat. When hot, stir to dissolve the sugar. Bring to a boil.

While the cream mixture is heating, place the remaining ¼ cup sugar and the egg yolks in the bowl of an electric mixer fitted with a paddle. Beat on high speed for 2 minutes until thoroughly combined, then use a rubber spatula to scrape down the sides of the bowl and the paddle. Beat on high for an additional 2 minutes until slightly thickened and pale yellow. If at this point the cream mixture has not yet started to boil, adjust the mixer speed to low and continue to mix until it does boil; otherwise, lumps may form when the boiling cream mixture is added.

Gradually pour the boiling cream mixture into the sugar and egg yolk mixture and mix on low to combine, about 1 minute. (To avoid splattering the boiling cream mixture, use a pouring shield attachment, or place a towel or plastic wrap over the top of the mixer and down the sides to the bowl.) Pour the combined mixture through a medium-gauge strainer into a clean medium saucepan, using a rubber spatula to transfer all of the mixture from the bowl. Heat over medium heat, stirring constantly. Bring to a temperature of 185°F, about 2 minutes. Use an instant-read thermometer for an accurate temperature reading of the mixture. Remove from the heat and transfer to a large stainless steel bowl. Cool the mixture in an ice water bath to a temperature of 40° to

45°F. Add the crème de menthe and stir to incorporate. Freeze in an ice cream machine, following the manufacturer's instructions. Just prior to removing the semifrozen ice cream from the machine, add the chocolate mini-morsels; churn for a few additional moments to fold the morsels into the ice cream.

BEGIN ASSEMBLING THE ICE CREAM SANDWICHES   Line the bottom and sides of 2 clean and dry 10¾ × 7 × 1½-inch nonstick biscuit/ brownie pans with plastic wrap. Portion half the amount of semifrozen ice cream into each pan. Use a rubber spatula to spread the ice cream evenly to the edges of each pan. Remove the cake layers from the refrigerator. Invert them onto the ice cream layer in each pan (shiny side up). Press down very gently on each cake layer to set it into place on the ice cream layer. Cover the top of each pan with plastic wrap and place in the freezer for 12 hours or overnight until the ice cream is firm to the touch.

AFTER 12 HOURS, FINISH THE ASSEMBLY   Remove the 2 pans with the frozen cake layers and ice cream from the freezer. Invert the frozen cake and ice cream sections onto a clean, dry work surface (the ice cream layers should be facing up). Remove the plastic wrap from the ice cream layers. Invert one of the cake and ice cream sections onto the other, and press down gently on the top cake layer so that both ice cream layers join as one (sounds a bit matrimonial, but it works). Remove and discard the plastic wrap from the top layer, then turn the 2 joined layers over to remove the remaining piece of plastic wrap. Place the joined layers into one of the pans, cover the top with plastic wrap, and place in the freezer for at least 2 hours before cutting and serving.

TO SERVE   Remove the pan with the joined layers from the freezer. Remove and discard the plastic wrap. Turn the frozen cake out onto a clean, dry cutting board. Use a sharp serrated slicer to trim the edges from the cake and ice cream to create an approximately 6-inch-wide by 9½-inch-long rectangle with smooth and even edges. Cut the rectangle in half lengthwise, then cut each section widthwise twice at about 3-inch intervals. Finally, cut each square in half diagonally for 12 sandwiches. Serve immediately, or individually wrap each sandwich in plastic wrap and store in a tightly sealed plastic container in the freezer.

THE CHEF'S TOUCH

Crème de menthe is defined by its vivid green color and assertive peppermint flavor. Dozens of spirits are called "crème de" something. Although different in flavor, from crème de banana to crème de violet, they share a sweetness that coats the tongue. Don't let the word *crème* mislead you; there is no cream in these liqueurs. They are, however, frequently combined with cream and put forth as a delicate cocktail.

If you enjoy the flavor of crème de menthe, but find the green color too loud, consider the widely available clear version of this liqueur (also simply called crème de menthe). On the other hand, if even greater technicolor is desired, add a drop or two of green food color to the cooled ice cream mixture along with the green crème de menthe just prior to transferring it to the ice cream machine.

The nonstick biscuit/brownie pans needed for this recipe seem to be an odd size; however, we did find them in the kitchenware department at the Target store in Williamsburg.

An astonishing 600-plus varieties of mint exist. Some are ornamental, but many have distinctive flavors and aromas and are suitable for cooking. With that many varieties it is not surprising that chocolate mint is among them. Remarkably, fresh chocolate mint smells exactly like a chocolate-covered peppermint wafer. Because we grow chocolate mint at Ganache Hill, we used it in the preparation of the Grasshopper Cake. You may substitute the same amount of spearmint or peppermint in the cake without making a significant taste difference in the baked cake.

The ice cream sandwich cakes may be prepared over 3 days.

DAY 1: Bake the Chocolate Grasshopper Cake layers. Once they're cooled, cover the cakes with plastic wrap and refrigerate until the next day.

DAY 2: Make the Crème de Menthe Ice Cream. Remove the cake layers from the refrigerator. Assemble as directed in the recipe. Cover the assembled cake and ice cream layers with plastic wrap and freeze until the next day.

DAY 3: Remove the cake and ice cream layers from the freezer. Finish the assembly as directed in the recipe, then return it to the freezer for 2 hours before cutting and serving. After assembly, you may keep the ice cream sandwich cake portions wrapped in plastic wrap in the freezer for several days. To avoid permeating the sandwiches with freezer odors, place them in a large, tightly sealed plastic container.

CHOCOLATE BRANDY SWIRL EGGNOG ICE CREAM

Unlike the cloying office-party prefabrication, this frosty rendition of eggnog brings cheer to the palate on the chilliest eve. Waves of brandy-saturated chocolate swirl through nutmeg-scented ice cream so divine you won't even miss the fruitcake.

MAKE THE CHOCOLATE BRANDY SWIRL Heat the corn syrup, 3 tablespoons of the brandy, and sugar in a small saucepan over medium heat. When hot, stir to dissolve the sugar. Bring to a boil. Adjust the heat and cook at a low boil, stirring occasionally, until the mixture reaches a temperature of 220°F, 5½ to 6 minutes. Use a candy thermometer versus an instant-read thermometer for an accurate temperature reading of the hot syrup. Remove the saucepan from the heat, then immediately add the semisweet chocolate and stir with a stainless steel kitchen spoon until dissolved. Add the remaining 3 tablespoons brandy and stir to incorporate. Pour the chocolate brandy syrup onto a baking sheet with sides, then refrigerate for 30 minutes. Remove the syrup from the refrigerator and hold at room temperature.

MAKE THE EGGNOG ICE CREAM Heat the heavy cream, half-and-half, ¼ cup of the sugar, and the nutmeg in a large saucepan over medium-high heat. When hot, stir to dissolve the sugar. Bring to a boil.

While the cream mixture is heating, place the egg yolks and the remaining ½ cup sugar in the bowl of an electric mixer fitted with a paddle. Beat on medium-high speed for 2 minutes until combined, then use a rubber spatula to scrape down the sides of the bowl. Beat on medium-high for an additional 2 minutes until slightly thickened and pale yellow. If at this point the cream mixture has not yet started to boil, adjust the mixer speed to low and continue to mix until it does boil; otherwise, lumps may form when the boiling cream mixture is added.

CHOCOLATE BRANDY SWIRL

⅓ cup light corn syrup

6 tablespoons brandy

3 tablespoons granulated sugar

4 ounces semisweet baking chocolate, coarsely chopped

EGGNOG ICE CREAM

2 cups heavy cream

1 cup half-and-half

¾ cup granulated sugar

1 teaspoon freshly grated nutmeg

6 large egg yolks

1 teaspoon pure vanilla extract

MAKES 1½ QUARTS

Gradually pour the boiling cream mixture into the yolk and sugar mixture and mix on low to combine, about 1 minute. (To avoid splattering the cream mixture, use a pouring shield attachment, or place a towel or plastic wrap over the top of the mixer and down the sides to the bowl.) Return the combined mixture to the saucepan, using a rubber spatula to transfer all of the mixture from the bowl.

Heat over medium heat, stirring constantly. Bring to a temperature of 185°F, about 3 minutes. Use an instant-read thermometer for an accurate temperature reading of the mixture. Remove from heat and transfer to a large stainless steel bowl. Cool in an ice water bath to 40° to 45°F.

When the mixture is cold, add the vanilla extract; stir to combine. Freeze in an ice cream machine following the manufacturer's instructions. Transfer about ⅓ of the semifrozen ice cream to a 2-quart plastic container. Add about ½ of the chilled chocolate brandy syrup. Repeat the layering by transferring about ⅓ more of the semifrozen ice cream and the remaining chocolate brandy syrup. Finish the layering with the remaining amount of ice cream. Swirl the ice cream by dipping the flat blade of a dinner knife into the semifrozen ice cream, and then lifting the blade of the knife out in a folding motion like the roll of a wave; repeat 6 to 10 times (depending on the swirliness desired) throughout the container of semifrozen ice cream. Securely cover the container, then place in the freezer for several hours before serving.

THE CHEF'S TOUCH

When I was a youngster growing up in the then primarily French Canadian–populated city of Woonsocket, Rhode Island, the midnight repast known as *réveillon* was celebrated in many homes following Midnight Mass. Chilled eggnog was the ubiquitous beverage served at these gatherings. In my home, this was served without spirits. Perhaps that is why I never developed a fondness for it until I was a chef at the Colonial Williamsburg Foundation. My friend Rolf Herion, then executive pastry chef of Colonial Williamsburg, served me his version on Christmas Eve. Rolf's eggnog, rich and brandy-infused, gave me a new take on the traditional drink. I hope our eggnog ice cream will do the same for you.

This ice cream is at its best when served within 5 days of preparation. Keep the container of ice cream securely covered in the freezer to prevent the ice cream from dehydrating and absorbing freezer odors.

CHOCOLATE SAY IT ISN'T CHEESECAKE ICE CREAM

This unconventional cream cheese–enhanced ice cream provides a perky twang that reminds me of cheesecake. The fact that chocolate in the form of ganache is the key flavor makes me smile and forget about any desire for cheesecake.

Place the semisweet chocolate in a medium bowl.

Heat the heavy cream and ¼ cup of the sugar in a small saucepan over medium-high heat. When hot, stir to dissolve the sugar. Bring to a boil. Pour the boiling cream mixture over the chopped chocolate, then stir with a whisk until smooth. Pour the mixture (a ganache by any other name is still a ganache) onto a nonstick baking sheet with sides and use a rubber spatula to spread the ganache in a smooth, even layer, to about 8 × 10 inches. Place the ganache in the refrigerator for 10 to 15 minutes, until cool.

Place the cream cheese and the remaining ½ cup sugar in the bowl of an electric mixer fitted with a paddle. Mix on low speed for 30 seconds to combine. Now beat on medium for 2 minutes, then use a rubber spatula to scrape down the sides of the bowl and the paddle. Continue beating the mixture on medium for an additional 2 minutes until very smooth. Scrape down the sides of the bowl and the paddle. Add the chilled ganache and mix on medium for 30 seconds. Operate the mixer on the lowest speed (stir) while gradually pouring in the half-and-half, milk, and vanilla extract; mix until thoroughly combined and smooth, about 1 minute. Remove the bowl from the mixer and use a rubber spatula to finish mixing the ingredients until thoroughly combined.

Freeze this mixture in an ice cream machine, following the manufacturer's instructions. Transfer the semifrozen ice cream to a 2-quart plastic container. Cover the container securely, then place in the freezer for several hours before serving.

8 ounces semisweet baking chocolate, coarsely chopped

¾ cup heavy cream

¾ cup granulated sugar

8 ounces cream cheese, cut into 1-ounce pieces

½ cup half-and-half

½ cup whole milk

1 teaspoon pure vanilla extract

MAKES SLIGHTLY MORE THAN
1 QUART

THE CHEF'S TOUCH

Use your fertile chocolate imagination to up the ante on this ice cream. The addition of chocolate chips or chocolate chunks (these are available at the supermarket, made by Baker's) to the semifrozen mixture would lend some additional texture, and it would double your chocolate money when the ice cream is ready to consume.

Partly because of the absence of eggs in this recipe, the ice cream may be very hard after being in the freezer for several hours. If it's difficult to scoop, place it in the refrigerator for 30 minutes or so before serving.

This ice cream is at its best when served within 3 to 4 days of preparation. Be certain to keep the container of ice cream securely covered in the freezer to prevent it from dehydrating and absorbing freezer odors.

GIANDUJA GONNA DO IT TO YA BIRTHDAY ICE CREAM

The word gianduja (zhahn-doo-yah) may seem inscrutable as well as unutterable, but it is a classic confection of hazelnut-flavored chocolate. In our recipe, we have infused a very smooth chocolate ice cream with hazelnut butter that contributes to creating a café-au-lait color as well as an extraordinary feeling of richness in your mouth. The crunch of the whole hazelnuts awakens you from the reverie that you have died and gone to heaven—well, almost!

Place 1 cup of the hazelnuts in the bowl of a food processor fitted with a metal blade. Process until completely liquified, about 3 minutes (stop the processor and scrape down the sides of the bowl after 2 minutes). Set aside.

Place the semisweet chocolate in a medium bowl and set aside.

Heat the heavy cream and the ¼ cup Frangelico in a small saucepan over medium-high heat. Bring to a boil. Pour the boiling cream mixture over the chopped chocolate, then stir with a whisk until smooth. Set the ganache aside.

Heat the half-and-half and ¼ cup of the sugar in a medium saucepan over medium heat. Stir to dissolve the sugar. Bring to a boil.

While the cream mixture is heating, place the remaining ½ cup sugar and the egg yolks in the bowl of an electric mixer fitted with a paddle. Beat on high speed for 2 minutes until thoroughly combined, then use a rubber spatula to scrape down the sides of the bowl. Beat on high for an additional 2 minutes until slightly thickened and pale yellow. If at this point the cream mixture has not yet started to boil, adjust the mixer speed to low and continue to mix until it does boil; otherwise, lumps may form when the boiling cream mixture is added.

Gradually pour the boiling cream mixture into the sugar and egg yolk mixture and mix on low to combine, about 45 seconds. (To avoid

2 cups skinned hazelnuts, toasted (see page 23)

6 ounces semisweet baking chocolate, coarsely chopped

½ cup heavy cream

¼ cup Frangelico (hazelnut-flavored liqueur) plus 2 tablespoons

1½ cups half-and-half

¾ cup granulated sugar

3 large eggs

MAKES 1¾ QUARTS

splattering the boiling mixture, use a pouring shield attachment, or place a towel or plastic wrap over the top of the mixer down the sides to the bowl.)

Return the combined mixture to the saucepan, using a rubber spatula to facilitate transferring all of the mixture from the bowl. Heat over medium heat, stirring constantly. Bring to a temperature of 185°F, about 2 minutes. Use an instant-read thermometer for an accurate temperature reading of the mixture. Remove from the heat and transfer to a large stainless steel bowl. Add the ganache and liquefied hazelnuts and stir to combine. Cool in an ice water bath to a temperature of 40° to 45°F. Add the remaining 2 tablespoons Frangelico and stir to combine. Freeze in an ice cream machine, following the manufacturer's instructions. Transfer the semifrozen ice cream to a 2-quart plastic container. Add the remaining 1 cup of hazelnuts and stir with a rubber spatula to evenly distribute. Securely cover the container, then place in the freezer for several hours before serving.

THE CHEF'S TOUCH

This ice cream is at its best when served within 5 to 6 days of preparation. Be certain to keep the container of ice cream securely covered in the freezer to prevent the ice cream from dehydrating and absorbing freezer odors.

RED, WHITE, AND BLUE BERRY ICE CREAM

It is a grand old flag that we celebrate here with an eye-popping parade of color. The purity of white chocolate marches with true-blue and red-cheeked berries for a mouth-filling explosion of flavor.

BEGIN PREPARING THE STARS AND STRIPES GARNISH Heat the sugar, water, and Wilderberry schnapps in a small saucepan over medium-high heat. When hot, stir to dissolve the sugar. Bring to a boil. Add the blueberries and stir to distribute. Adjust the heat to simmer the mixture for 6 minutes until the blueberries are very soft. Remove from the heat, then strain the blueberries, discarding the liquid. Transfer the blueberries to a dinner plate and spread evenly, let them cool, then place in the freezer.

MAKE THE WHITE CHOCOLATE ICE CREAM Heat the white chocolate and ½ cup of the half-and-half in the top half of a double boiler, or in a medium glass bowl in a microwave oven (see pages 20–21), and stir until the chocolate has melted and the mixture is smooth. Set aside.

Heat the heavy cream, the remaining 1 cup half-and-half, and ⅓ cup of the granulated sugar in a medium saucepan over medium-high heat. When hot, stir to dissolve the sugar. Bring to a boil.

While the cream mixture is heating, place the remaining ⅓ cup sugar and the egg yolks in the bowl of an electric mixer fitted with a paddle. Beat on high speed for 2 minutes until thoroughly combined, then use a rubber spatula to scrape down the sides of the bowl. Beat on high for an additional 2 minutes until slightly thickened and pale yellow. If at this point the heavy cream mixture has not yet started to boil, adjust the mixer speed to low and continue to mix until it does boil; otherwise, lumps may form when the boiling cream mixture is added.

Gradually pour the boiling cream mixture into the sugar and egg

STARS AND STRIPES GARNISH

¼ cup granulated sugar

¼ cup water

¼ cup Wilderberry schnapps

1 cup fresh blueberries, stemmed and rinsed

1½ cups fresh red raspberries, rinsed

¼ teaspoon red food color

¼ teaspoon blue food color

WHITE CHOCOLATE ICE CREAM

6 ounces white chocolate, coarsely chopped

1½ cups half-and-half

1½ cups heavy cream

⅔ cup granulated sugar

3 large egg yolks

MAKES **2** QUARTS

yolk mixture and mix on low to combine, about 45 seconds. (To avoid splattering the cream mixture, use a pouring shield attachment, or place a towel or plastic wrap over the top of the mixer down the sides to the bowl.) Return the combined mixture to the saucepan, using a rubber spatula to facilitate transferring all of the mixture from the bowl. Heat over medium heat, stirring constantly. Bring to a temperature of 185°F, about 2½ minutes. Use an instant-read thermometer for an accurate temperature reading of the mixture. Remove from the heat and transfer to a large stainless steel bowl. Add the white chocolate and half-and-half mixture and stir to combine. Cool in an ice water bath to a temperature of 40° to 45°F. Freeze in an ice cream machine, following the manufacturer's instructions.

ASSEMBLE THE RED, WHITE, AND BLUE BERRY ICE CREAM
Just prior to removing the White Chocolate Ice Cream from the ice cream machine, place the raspberries and red food color in a medium bowl. Remove the blueberries from the freezer and place them in a separate medium bowl along with the blue food color. Transfer 1 cup of the semifrozen ice cream into the bowl with the raspberries and 1 cup into the bowl with the blueberries. Use a rubber spatula to combine the ice cream in each bowl with its respective fruit and food color until incorporated (try to do this as quickly as possible to prevent the ice cream from melting too much).

Now transfer the red raspberry ice cream to a 2-quart plastic container. Remove the remaining white chocolate ice cream from the ice cream machine and place it on top of the red raspberry ice cream. Finally, place the blueberry ice cream on the top of the white chocolate ice cream. Swirl the ice cream by dipping the flat blade of a cake spatula into the semifrozen ice cream, then lifting the blade of the spatula out of the semifrozen ice cream in a folding motion like the roll of a wave; repeat 4 to 6 times (depending on the swirliness desired) throughout the container of semifrozen ice cream. Securely cover the container, then place in the freezer for several hours before serving.

𝒯HE CHEF'S TOUCH
Can't find Wilderberry schnapps? Then select another berry liqueur.

This ice cream is at its best when served within 3 to 4 days of preparation. Keep the container of ice cream securely covered in the freezer to prevent it from dehydrating and absorbing freezer odors.

Cocoa Mint-Julep Pop

By law, our pops are not for kiddos! More refreshing than intoxicating, these frozen concoctions, not too sweet, with a taste of cocoa and a hint of bourbon, are just right for a summertime grown-up gathering.

Heat the water, sugar, and cocoa powder in a medium saucepan over medium-high heat. When hot, stir to dissolve the sugar and cocoa. Bring to a simmer. Remove from the heat and transfer to a large stainless steel bowl. Cool in an ice water bath to a temperature of 40° to 45°F. When the mixture is cold, add the bourbon and mint. Stir to disperse. Freeze in an ice cream machine, following the manufacturer's instructions. Evenly divide the semifrozen mixture into four 8-ounce clear plastic cups. Use the back of a teaspoon to smooth the mixture evenly. Insert a wooden pop stick in the center and 3/4 of the way down into the semifrozen mixture in each cup. Cover the top of each cup with plastic wrap, then place the cups in the freezer for several hours until very hard.

When ready to serve, remove the frozen pops from the freezer. By pushing up with your thumbs from the bottom of the cup while holding the rim with your fingers, you should be able to release the pop from the cup without much effort. If the pop does not release effortlessly wrap a damp, warm towel around the sides of the cup and hold it there for 4 to 6 seconds. The pop will then slip out of the cup. Eat or serve immediately in the cup.

3 cups water

½ cup granulated sugar

¼ cup unsweetened cocoa
   powder

3 tablespoons bourbon

1 tablespoon coarsely
   chopped fresh mint

MAKES 4 POPS

The Chef's Touch

Although some gardeners disdain mint for its invasive nature, I have always enjoyed its presence in the garden at Ganache Hill. The robust fragrance of fresh mint is a pleasing aspect of this versatile herb. I also like the fact that it is so easily transplantable; a slight tug and you have stem and root system in hand. Of the four different varieties of mint—spearmint, peppermint, orange mint, and chocolate mint—growing in our herb garden, it is the latter, as you might imagine, that I find irresistible. Whatever fresh mint you decide upon for this recipe, select mint that has sprightly green leaves and few blemishes.

You probably will have trouble finding Popsicle sticks at the supermarket. Popsicle is a registered brand name, and to my knowledge, if you want a Popsicle stick, you will have to purchase a frozen Popsicle, not such a bad thing on a sweltering day. Look for wooden pop sticks, also called craft sticks, in the toy aisle at your local supermarket, drugstore, or anywhere else that sells craft materials.

If presenting a Cocoa Mint-Julep Pop in a clear plastic cup seems a bit prosaic, use fancy frozen pop molds, which are available from kitchenware purveyors such as Sur La Table (see Online Sources, page 161).

After assembly, you may keep the Cocoa Mint-Julep Pop portions in the clear plastic cups, each tightly wrapped in plastic wrap, in the freezer for several days.

FROZEN CHOCOLATE OH-HONEY SO-FLUFFY MOUSSE BOMBE

Not your typical *bombe glacée* with different layers of ice cream and fruit, our bombe is the creation of Ganache Hill test kitchen chef Brett Bailey. Brett was looking for an airy texture to be the core of this dessert, so he decided to work with mousse rather than ice cream. We are always striving to bring different textures together, and in this cake the pecan-embellished mousse, contrasting with the smooth chocolate honey mousse, works a certain magic with the truffle cake and the chocolate honey glaze. The appearance is drop-dead gorgeous; the half a cannonball-like shape enrobed with a honey enhanced chocolate glaze which, until cut, keeps the secret of the frozen chocolate and pecan mousse interior positioned on the densest chocolate truffle cake imaginable.

MAKE THE CHOCOLATE TRUFFLE CAKE Preheat the oven to 300°F.

Assemble a 9 × 2-inch nonstick springform pan with the bottom insert turned over (the lip of the insert facing down). Lightly coat the inside of the pan with some of the melted butter. Line the bottom of the pan with parchment paper (or wax paper), then lightly coat the paper with more melted butter. Set aside.

Melt the semisweet chocolate, the ¼ pound butter, and the unsweetened chocolate in the top half of a double boiler or in a small glass bowl in the microwave oven (see pages 20–21), and stir until smooth. Set aside until needed.

Place the eggs, egg yolk, and sugar in the bowl of an electric mixer fitted with a balloon whip. Whisk on high speed until light in color and slightly thickened, about 5 minutes. Remove the bowl from the mixer. Using a rubber spatula (which won't overaerate the mixture), fold the

CHOCOLATE TRUFFLE CAKE

1 teaspoon unsalted butter, melted

¼ pound (1 stick) unsalted butter, cut into ½-ounce pieces

6 ounces semisweet baking chocolate, coarsely chopped

2 ounces unsweetened baking chocolate, coarsely chopped

2 large eggs

1 large egg yolk

1 tablespoon granulated sugar

CHOCOLATE SO-FLUFFY MOUSSE

8 ounces semisweet baking chocolate, coarsely chopped

¼ cup warm water

¼ cup honey

4 tablespoons granulated sugar

3 large egg whites

2 cups heavy cream

1½ cups pecan halves,
    toasted (see page 23)
    (1 cup coarsely chopped
    and ½ cup of the best-
    looking halves reserved
    for garnish)

CHOCOLATE OH-HONEY
GLAZE

8 ounces semisweet baking
    chocolate, coarsely
    chopped

½ cup heavy cream

¼ cup honey

2 tablespoons unsalted
    butter

SERVES 8

chocolate and butter mixture into the egg and sugar mixture. Pour this batter into the prepared pan and spread evenly. Place the pan on a baking sheet on the center rack of the oven. Bake for 26 minutes, until a toothpick inserted in the center of the cake comes out ever so slightly moist with dark chocolate crumbs. Remove the cake from the oven and cool in the pan at room temperature for 20 minutes. Release the cake from the pan and invert it onto a cake circle (or a cake plate). Remove the bottom insert, then carefully peel the parchment paper away. Set aside at room temperature.

MAKE THE CHOCOLATE SO-FLUFFY MOUSSE   Melt 5 ounces of the chopped semisweet chocolate in the top half of a double boiler or in a small glass bowl in the microwave oven (see pages 20–21), and stir until smooth. Set aside until needed.

Measure the warm water into a Pyrex measuring cup and add the honey. Transfer the water and honey to a small saucepan; add 2 tablespoons of the sugar. Bring to a boil over medium-high heat. Boil the mixture, stirring occasionally, until it reaches 240°F (for the candy makers, this is the soft-ball stage), 5 to 6 minutes. I recommend using a candy thermometer versus an instant-read thermometer for an accurate temperature reading of the hot syrup. Remove the saucepan from the heat, then immediately place the egg whites and the remaining 2 tablespoons sugar in the bowl of an electric mixer fitted with a balloon whip. Whisk on high speed until soft peaks form, about 1 minute. Carefully and slowly add the screaming-hot honey mixture to the egg white and sugar mixture while whisking on high speed until the mixture is very thick, about 4 minutes. Remove the bowl from the mixer. Add the melted semisweet chocolate and stir with a rubber spatula to incorporate. In a clean, dry bowl whisk the heavy cream on medium-high speed until stiff peaks form, about 1½ minutes. Use a rubber spatula to fold the whipped cream into the chocolate honey meringue until uniformly light chocolate in color. Refrigerate for a few minutes.

Melt the remaining 3 ounces chopped semisweet chocolate in the top half of a double boiler or in a small glass bowl in the microwave oven (see pages 20–21), and stir until smooth. Transfer the melted chocolate into a well-chilled large bowl. Add 2 cups of the chocolate honey mousse and the 1 cup chopped pecans. Use a rubber spatula to fold the ingredients together until combined. Refrigerate until needed.

BEGIN THE ASSEMBLY OF THE BOMBE   Lightly spray the inside of a large glass or stainless steel bowl (the bowl should be 9 to 9¼ inches across the top) with a pure vegetable pan coating. Line the inside of the bowl with plastic wrap. Transfer the chocolate honey mousse to the bowl. Use a rubber spatula to spread evenly (to eliminate air pockets) and smoothly (to create a flat surface). Pour the chocolate honey pecan mousse on top of the first mousse layer and once again spread evenly and smoothly. Place the truffle cake layer on top of the chocolate honey pecan mousse layer and gently but firmly press down on the cake until it is level with the mousse (the pressing down is important to avoid a gap between the cake layer and the mousse layer). Cover the bowl with plastic wrap. Place the bowl in the freezer for at least 6 hours or overnight.

MAKE THE CHOCOLATE OH-HONEY GLAZE   Place the chopped semisweet chocolate in a medium bowl.

Heat the heavy cream, honey, and butter in a small saucepan over medium-high heat. When hot, stir to combine. Bring to a boil. Pour the boiling cream mixture over the chocolate. Stir with a whisk until smooth.

Place a cooling rack on a baking sheet with sides.

Remove the bombe from the freezer. Remove and discard the plastic wrap over the bowl. Invert the bombe onto a cake circle. Wrap a damp, hot cotton towel around the sides of the bowl and hold it there for 30 seconds. Remove the bowl and the plastic wrap from the bombe. Slide the bombe off the cake circle onto the cooling rack. Pour the chocolate honey glaze over the bombe, allowing the flowing glaze to coat the entire surface. Use a utility turner (wide spatula) to transfer the bombe onto a cake circle (or cake plate). Place the bombe in the freezer for 20 minutes. Refrigerate the glaze remaining on the sheet tray for 20 minutes.

Transfer the chilled glaze from the baking sheet to a pastry bag fitted with a medium star tip. Remove the bombe from the freezer. Pipe a circle of columns, each one touching the next, alternating between a ½-inch- and 1½-inch-high column, from the bottom edge of the bombe toward the top. The columns should be about ¾ inch wide. Place a pecan half on the bottom edge of every other column of glaze. Place the bombe in the freezer for 30 minutes before cutting and serving.

TO SERVE   Heat the blade of a serrated slicer under hot running water and wipe the blade dry before cutting each slice. Serve immediately.

𝒯HE CHEF'S TOUCH

Turning over the bottom insert of the springform pan (the lip of the bottom insert facing down) before assembling the pan will make it easier to remove the insert from the baked cake.

For this recipe, avoid the exotically flavored single-flower honeys and select a mild-flavored clover or orange blossom honey.

Make certain that the top of the bowl you use to assemble the bombe is 9 to 9¼ inches across. The truffle cake, which is baked in a 9 × 2-inch springform pan, will be approximately 9 inches after baking. If you have a bowl that is slightly smaller in diameter, you may trim the cake so it will fit. If your bowl is more than 9¼ inches, you can either go out and purchase the correct size bowl or skip this recipe (I would invest in a new bowl).

This dessert may be prepared over 3 days.

DAY 1: Bake the Chocolate Truffle Cake. Once it's baked, cool to room temperature. Release the cake from the pan as directed in the recipe. Cover the cake with plastic wrap and refrigerate until the next day.

DAY 2: Make the Chocolate So-Fluffy Mousse. Begin the assembly of the bombe as directed in the recipe and place the bowl in the freezer overnight.

DAY 3: Make the Chocolate Oh-Honey Glaze. Remove the bombe from the bowl. Cover and garnish the bombe as directed. Freeze for 30 minutes before serving.

After assembly, you may keep the mousse bombe in the freezer for several days. To avoid permeating the bombe with freezer odors, place it in a large, tightly sealed plastic container.

MOUSSES, CANDIES, AND OTHER CHOCOLATE TREATS

So it's not your birthday, anniversary, Thanksgiving, or wedding day. It's just a good time to celebrate chocolate (and when isn't it?) with an out-of-sight confection. This treasury of mousses, pies, candies, tarts, and even French toast will make any occasion a party.

COCOA BERRY YOGURT MOUSSE

FROSTED STRAWBERRIES
12 large fresh strawberries
¼ cup granulated sugar

COCOA YOGURT MOUSSE
½ cup confectioners' sugar
½ cup unsweetened cocoa powder
1 cup heavy cream
1 cup plain lowfat yogurt

SERVES 4

Yogurt brings the tang, strawberries the texture and sweetness, cocoa the raison d'être, and the heavy cream the voluptuousness.

FROST THE STRAWBERRIES Place the strawberries in a colander and spray with lukewarm water. Gently shake the colander to remove excess water. Stem and then cut the berries widthwise into ¼-inch-thick slices. Place the berries in a medium noncorrosive bowl. Sprinkle the sugar over the berries, then toss gently to combine. Equally divide the strawberries among four 8- to 10-ounce glasses, cups, or whatever you desire for presentation (the vessel chosen should be noncorrosive). Set aside at room temperature.

MAKE THE COCOA YOGURT MOUSSE In a sifter combine the confectioners' sugar and cocoa powder. Sift onto a large piece of parchment paper (or wax paper) and set aside.

Place the heavy cream in the bowl of an electric mixer fitted with a balloon whip. Operate the mixer on low speed while gradually adding the dry ingredients; mix until incorporated, about 1 minute. Use a rubber spatula to scrape down the sides of the bowl. Now whisk on medium for 5 seconds. Remove the bowl from the mixer. Add the yogurt; fold the ingredients together with a rubber spatula until thoroughly combined. Immediately spoon the yogurt mousse onto the strawberries in each glass (a bit more than ½ cup in each). Serve immediately, or cover the top of each glass with plastic wrap and refrigerate for up to 24 hours before serving.

THE CHEF'S TOUCH
Strawberries are just the tip of an iceberg of possibilities for this quickie dessert, as many other berries would work well, either fresh or frozen. If you select frozen fruit, merely thaw it, then portion it along with natural juices into the serving dish. No need to sprinkle with sugar unless the fruit is fresh.

CHOCOLATE APRICOT PUDDING MOUSSE PERFECTIONS WITH CHOCOLATE-DRENCHED CASHEWS

Parfait, a French word meaning "perfect," is also a classic French dessert. Layers of whipped cream, custard, and fruit puree are arranged alternately in a special *parfait* mold, which is then frozen. In the United States, a parfait is usually an ice cream dessert presented in a tall, narrow glass. Just for the heck of it, we decided to call our dessert a Perfection, because who is going to argue with the French about the proper presentation of one of their classics? *Pas moi*, I'd rather eat chocolate.

This dessert is a circus of delightful flavors dancing on your tongue. Boldly sweet dried apricots first get tipsy on hazelnut-flavored liqueur, then plunge into a dense chocolate pudding mousse before cartwheeling to the crunch of chocolate-coated cashews. Send in the clowns!

PREPARE THE APRICOT COMPOTATION Heat the apricots, Frangelico, and water in a medium saucepan over medium heat. Bring to a boil, stirring occasionally while the mixture is heating. Reduce the heat to low and simmer the mixture, stirring occasionally, until most of the liquid has evaporated, leaving a small amount of syrup in the bottom of the saucepan, about 14 minutes. Remove from the heat. Transfer the apricots and syrup to a baking sheet with sides and spread evenly. Refrigerate the apricots until needed.

MAKE THE CHOCOLATE PUDDING MOUSSE Melt the semisweet chocolate in the top half of a double boiler or in a large glass bowl in a

APRICOT COMPOTATION

2 cups dried apricots, cut into quarters

½ cup Frangelico (hazelnut-flavored liqueur)

½ cup water

CHOCOLATE PUDDING MOUSSE

8 ounces semisweet baking chocolate, coarsely chopped

1⅔ cups half-and-half

¼ cup granulated sugar

2 tablespoons cornstarch

2 tablespoons water

1 cup heavy cream

⅓ cup confectioners' sugar, sifted

**6 ounces semisweet baking
  chocolate, coarsely
  chopped**

**1¼ cups whole cashews,
  toasted (see page 23)**

MAKES 4 LARGE PERFECTIONS

microwave oven (see pages 20–21), and stir until smooth. Set aside until needed. If the chocolate was melted in a double boiler, transfer the chocolate to a large glass bowl. Set aside.

Heat the half-and-half and sugar in a medium saucepan over medium heat, stirring to dissolve the sugar. Bring to a boil, then reduce to a simmer. As soon as the cream is simmering, whisk together the cornstarch and water in a small bowl until the cornstarch is dissolved and the mixture is smooth. Gradually drizzle the cornstarch mixture into the simmering cream, stirring with a whisk until the cream has slightly thickened, about 20 seconds. Reduce the heat to low and simmer for 2 minutes, stirring constantly with a rubber spatula (the rubber spatula will help prevent the thickened cream from sticking to the bottom of the saucepan and scorching). Pour the cream into the bowl of chocolate and whisk vigorously until thoroughly combined. Transfer the chocolate pudding to a baking sheet with sides and spread evenly toward the edges; refrigerate for 15 minutes, until the mixture is no longer hot, but isn't cold, either (if the mixture is cold throughout, it will not incorporate properly in the next step). As soon as the pudding is no longer hot, remove from the refrigerator and set aside.

Place the heavy cream and confectioners' sugar in the bowl of an electric mixer fitted with a balloon whip. Mix on low speed for 15 seconds, then increase the speed to medium-high and whisk until soft peaks form, about 1 minute and 15 seconds. Add the chocolate pudding and whisk on medium until combined, about 15 seconds. Remove the bowl from the mixer and use a rubber spatula to finish mixing the chocolate pudding mousse until thoroughly combined (this should yield about 4 cups). Cover with plastic wrap and refrigerate.

MAKE THE CHOCOLATE-DRENCHED CASHEWS Melt the semisweet chocolate in the top half of a double boiler or in a medium glass bowl in a microwave oven (see pages 20–21), and stir until smooth. Add the cashews and stir until the cashews are drenched with the chocolate. Transfer the chocolate-drenched cashews to a baking sheet lined with parchment paper (or wax paper) and spread the nuts into as even a layer as possible. Refrigerate for 20 minutes, until the chocolate is hard.

Coarsely chop the cashews with a cook's knife and set aside (this should yield slightly more than 2 cups).

ASSEMBLE THE PERFECTIONS   To assemble the Perfections, fill a pastry bag fitted with a large straight tip (#9 with a ¾-inch opening) with the Chocolate Pudding Mousse. Place about 1 heaping tablespoon of the cashews in the bottom of each of four 16-ounce glasses. Next, place about 1 slightly heaping tablespoon of the Apricot Compotation on top of the cashews in each glass. Pipe an even layer of about ¼ cup of the pudding mousse on top of the apricots in each glass.

Follow the same sequence of layers as you fill the glasses, increasing the ingredients for the second layer to about 2 heaping tablespoons cashews, about 2 slightly heaping tablespoons apricots, and about ⅓ cup pudding mousse. For the third and final layer, use about 2 heaping tablespoons cashews and about 2 level tablespoons apricots, and evenly distribute the remaining pudding mousse in each glass. Garnish each of the Perfections with 1 heaping tablespoon cashews and a sprinkle of the remaining apricots. Cover the top of each glass with plastic wrap and refrigerate for 1 hour before serving.

*T*HE CHEF'S TOUCH

I find the deep orange blush of a dried apricot, and its sweet with a slightly tart taste, compelling. When fresh, the diminutive apricot yields succulent, sweet flesh. Unfortunately, fresh apricots begin a descent in quality not long after being plucked from the tree. If you have access to exquisitely fresh apricots, by all means use them in this recipe (wash, dry, don't peel, pit, then cut into slices). But don't get them drunk on the Frangelico; rather, sprinkle the slices with the liqueur just moments prior to the assembly of the Perfections.

I prefer the dried whole Turkish apricots over the dried apricot halves from California.

Frangelico is a hazelnut-flavored liqueur produced in Italy. It is not overly sweet, and the fusion of flavors from the wild hazelnuts, berries, and flowers used in the crafting of this very pleasant liqueur are subtle enough that it may be enjoyed as a beverage (a snifter of Frangelico served with the Perfections would certainly elicit an exclamation of *Parfait!* from your guests) as well as a dessert component.

Why not use hazelnuts for the Perfections rather than cashews? You certainly may, but for this confection, I prefer the profound buttery flavor of the cashews.

We decided to use 16-ounce glasses for dramatic effect (and because more chocolate is better). Ten- to 12-ounce glasses may also be used. I suggest finding some exotic-looking glasses and having fun with the presentation. Of course, the smaller the glass, the more portions this recipe will produce.

For easy entertaining, all the components for the Perfections may be prepared early in the day or, for that matter, the day before. Prepare each item as directed in the recipe, then refrigerate until ready to assemble.

Once each Perfection is assembled, cover the top with plastic wrap and refrigerate for up to 24 hours before serving.

TOOT, TOOT, TOOT C-ROLL

If this fudge roll does not remind you of a beloved candy counter treat, I suggest that confectionery therapy may be in order. This sweet thing is going to tie up your mouth with more delightful chews than your Toot-C ever dreamed of.

Heat the brown sugar, heavy cream, corn syrup, and unsweetened chocolate in a medium saucepan over medium heat. When hot, stir to dissolve the sugar and melt the chocolate. Bring to a boil. Once the mixture begins to boil, use a rubber spatula to scrape down the sides of the saucepan, then allow the mixture to boil undisturbed (do not stir, as stirring will create sugar crystals) until it reaches 240°F (for the candy makers, this is the soft-ball stage), 4½ to 5 minutes (use a candy thermometer for an accurate reading). Remove the saucepan from the heat. Add the butter, a ¼-ounce piece at a time, stirring with a wooden spoon to incorporate before adding the next piece of butter. Add the vanilla extract and stir to incorporate.

Transfer this fudge mixture to the bowl of an electric mixer fitted with a paddle, then add the granola and beat on medium for exactly 3 minutes until very thick. Remove the bowl from the mixer and use a rubber spatula to scrape down the sides of the bowl and the paddle. Transfer the fudge mixture to an 18 × 12-inch piece of parchment paper (or wax paper). Although the fudge mixture is still warm, it's time to roll (if the mixture is allowed to cool, it will be difficult to roll into shape). With the palms of both hands, roll the fudge into a very compact cylinder about 15 inches long and 2 inches in diameter. Roll the paper around the cylinder, then place on a baking sheet and refrigerate for 1½ hours until cold and very firm.

Remove the fudge roll from the refrigerator and discard the paper. Use a serrated knife or slicer to cut the roll into 30 individual ½-inch-thick slices. Although the Toot, Toot, Toot C-Roll slices may be devoured

2 cups (1 pound) tightly packed light brown sugar

½ cup heavy cream

¼ cup light corn syrup

4 ounces unsweetened baking chocolate, coarsely chopped

1½ ounces unsalted butter, cut into ¼-ounce pieces

2 teaspoons pure vanilla extract

1½ cups granola

MAKES 30 SLICES

immediately, I suggest keeping them at room temperature for about 20 minutes or so before serving to optimize the flavor.

$\mathcal{T}$HE CHEF'S TOUCH

We were not fussy about the selection of granola for this recipe. Brett picked it from a bin in the bulk food section at the supermarket.

The sliced Toot, Toot, Toot C-Rolls will retain all of their chocolaty, chewy charm for several days if you keep them stored in a tightly sealed plastic container at room temperature. For long-term storage, up to several weeks, the sliced rolls may be frozen in a tightly sealed plastic container to prevent dehydration and to protect them from freezer odors.

WHITE RUSSIANS

A bite of chocolate heaven, or perhaps for the more delicate eater, a nibble or two. This pleasurable orb, inspired by a classic cocktail, may not intoxicate, but it is certain to sate the most lustful chocolate lover.

MAKE THE WHITE RUSSIAN GANACHE Place the semisweet chocolate in a medium bowl. Heat the heavy cream, Kahlúa, and vodka in a small saucepan over medium heat. Bring to a boil. Pour the boiling cream mixture over the chopped chocolate, then stir with a whisk until smooth. Pour the mixture (it can now be labeled as ganache, and an exceptionally aromatic ganache at that) onto a nonstick baking sheet with sides and use a rubber spatula to spread the ganache in a smooth, even rectangle about 8 × 10 inches. Place the ganache in the freezer for 15 minutes, or in the refrigerator for 25 to 30 minutes, until very firm to the touch.

Remove the ganache from the freezer or the refrigerator. Line a baking sheet with parchment paper (or wax paper). Portion 10 level tablespoons (½ ounce each) of ganache onto the paper. Wearing a pair of disposable vinyl (or latex) gloves, individually roll each portion of ganache in your palms in a circular motion, using just enough gentle pressure to form a smooth orb. Now you have a truffle, albeit an unadorned one, but adornment is soon to follow. Return each formed truffle onto the paper-lined baking sheet, and place in the freezer for 30 minutes.

PREPARE THE BITTERSWEET CHOCOLATE COATING AND ASSEMBLE THE WHITE RUSSIANS Line a baking sheet with parchment paper or wax paper.

Heat the bittersweet chocolate in a small glass bowl in a microwave oven set at medium power for 1 minute and 20 seconds. Remove the chocolate from the microwave oven, then use a rubber spatula to con-

WHITE RUSSIAN GANACHE
4 ounces semisweet baking chocolate, coarsely chopped
¼ cup heavy cream
1 tablespoon Kahlúa
1½ teaspoons vodka

BITTERSWEET CHOCOLATE COATING
6 ounces bittersweet baking chocolate, coarsely chopped

MAKES **10** TRUFFLES

stantly stir the chocolate until it no longer appears to be melting, about 3 minutes. (The consistency of the partially melted chocolate will be thick, and probably several pieces of chocolate will not have melted completely. If the chocolate is completely smooth after being stirred, it probably got too hot—try again with 6 more ounces of coarsely chopped chocolate for a few seconds less time in the microwave.) Return the bowl of stirred chocolate to the microwave for an additional 20 seconds on medium power. Remove the chocolate and constantly stir with a rubber spatula until the chocolate is completely smooth and free of lumps, about 30 seconds.

Remove the truffles from the freezer. Wearing a pair of disposable vinyl (or latex) gloves, individually submerse the truffles in the tempered chocolate (moving quickly so the melted chocolate does not stiffen), then place the chocolate-coated truffles on the parchment-lined baking sheet. Transfer any remaining tempered chocolate to a small plastic zippered bag. Snip the tip from a bottom corner of the bag. Pipe a small amount of chocolate in a zigzag pattern over the top of each truffle. Allow the bittersweet chocolate coating on the truffles to harden at air-conditioned room temperature (68° to 78°F) (or in the refrigerator) before serving.

THE CHEF'S TOUCH

The provenance of the White Russian cocktail is illusive. Rather than concoct an apocryphal history for this delicious beverage, I would prefer to pass on my favorite recipe for said drink: 2½ ounces premium vodka, 1½ ounces Kahlúa, and 1 ounce heavy cream poured into a double old-fashioned glass filled with ice, and stirred.

Instead of a tablespoon to measure the ganache for the truffles, you may use a level #70 ice cream scoop.

A light dusting of unsweetened powdered cocoa sprinkled onto the truffles before the bittersweet chocolate coating has firmed would be an agreeable finishing touch.

The White Russians may be held at room temperature for several hours before serving. If you are not planning to serve the truffles on the day that they were prepared, I would suggest refrigerating in a tightly sealed plastic container for up to 3 days. Remove the truffles from the refrigerator 2 to 3 hours before serving.

CHOCOLATE-IN-PARADISE
TOASTED ALMOND BARK

A simple candy that's ideal for holiday gift giving.

Line a baking sheet with sides with parchment paper.

Combine the dried fruit in a small bowl.

Place the almonds in a large bowl. Pour the melted chocolate over the almonds and use a rubber spatula to combine. Transfer the chocolate and almond mixture to the lined baking sheet. Use a rubber spatula (or an offset spatula) to spread the mixture as evenly as possible into a rectangle approximately 8 × 12. Sprinkle the dried fruit uniformly over the entire surface of the chocolate and almond mixture. Use the palms of your hands to gently press the fruit into the chocolate.

Cover the baking sheet with plastic wrap and refrigerate until the bark is hard, about 30 minutes. Remove the baking sheet from the refrigerator and transfer the bark to a cutting board. Use a cook's knife to cut the bark into pieces the size you want. Refrigerate in a tightly sealed plastic container.

1/3 cup dried apricots, cut into 1/4-inch pieces

1/3 cup dried mangoes, cut into 1/4-inch pieces

1/3 cup dried papayas, cut into 1/4-inch pieces

1/3 cup dried pineapples, cut into 1/4-inch pieces

1 1/2 cups whole toasted almonds

12 ounces semisweet baking chocolate, coarsely chopped and melted (see pages 20–21)

MAKES 1 3/4 POUNDS

THE CHEF'S TOUCH

This simple candy was the hit of our "hands-on, no-holds-barred, all-chocolate cooking class" at the Mauna Lani Bay Hotel on the island of Hawaii for the Cuisines of the Sun held in July 2001. I was there as guest chef along with Ganache Hill test kitchen chef Brett Bailey and Trellis head pastry chef Kelly Bailey. I can sum up the class by saying there was chocolate everywhere.

Because the chocolate for this bark is not tempered, it is a messy albeit delectable affair if you attempt to eat it out of hand. I won't dissuade you from doing that, but I suggest that you chop the bark into 1/2-inch or so pieces once it is cold, then sprinkle it over your favorite chocolate ice cream (especially superb over white chocolate ice cream, page 127).

For a clean cut and properly diced pieces of dried fruit, use a serrated stainless steel cook's knife.

You say you don't have a serrated stainless steel cook's knife and anyway you are not in the mood to dice dried fruit? Then I suggest the Sun-Maid Tropical Medley available at most supermarkets. Each 7-ounce package contains a mix of the fruit we list for this recipe with 2 to 3 more to boot.

PEANUT BUTTERY CHOCOLATE PEANUT BRITTLE

Your ivories are in for a workout with this peanut-laden chocolate candy. Yes, it is called brittle, but it's not soft on flavor. Every molar-numbing bite of peanut butter, peanuts, and chocolate is fused together by caramelized sugar. Just keep chewing, but carefully.

Place the sugar and lemon juice in a large saucepan. Stir with a long-handled metal kitchen spoon to combine. (The sugar will resemble moist sand.)

Caramelize the sugar for about 10 minutes over medium-high heat, stirring constantly with the spoon to break up any lumps. The sugar will first turn clear as it liquefies, then light brown as it caramelizes. Remove the saucepan from the heat, add the unsweetened chocolate, and stir until melted and incorporated. Now add the peanut butter and butter and stir until incorporated and smooth. Add the peanuts and stir until combined.

Immediately transfer the extremely hot mixture (be careful in handling!) to a 10 × 15-inch baking sheet with sides. Use an offset spatula to spread the mixture evenly and as close to the edges of the baking sheet as possible (it should cover most of the surface, unless you dawdled and took too much time in the spreading, which left you with a large lump of brittle rather than a sheet). Harden at room temperature for at least 30 minutes.

Invert the brittle onto a clean, dry cutting board. (It should pop right out of the baking sheet.) Use your hands to break the brittle into pieces the size you want. Store the brittle, with parchment paper (or wax paper) between the layers to prevent sticking, in a tightly sealed plastic container until you are ready to dispatch it.

2 cups granulated sugar

1 teaspoon fresh lemon juice

2 ounces unsweetened baking chocolate, coarsely chopped

1/2 cup creamy peanut butter

1 ounce unsalted butter, cut into 1/2-ounce pieces

1 1/2 cups unsalted dry-roasted peanuts

MAKES SLIGHTLY SOUTH OF 2 POUNDS

THE CHEF'S TOUCH

Ganache Hill test kitchen chef Brett Bailey used what seemed like a truckload of sugar perfecting this recipe. Brett was in search of what he labels the ideal brittle—one that has an abundance of chocolate and peanuts and does not yield to a gentle bite. Brett can afford to be so enamored of this type of candy, as his brother Jeff is a dentist.

The Peanut Buttery Chocolate Peanut Brittle will keep for several days at air-conditioned room temperature (68° to 78°F) if stored in a tightly sealed plastic container, or in the freezer for several weeks. To prevent your brittle from fusing into a solid mass, make sure to place sheets of parchment paper (or wax paper) between the pieces.

MOCHA SAMBUCA SHOOTERS

These Lilliputian cakes deliver Herculean flavor. Here, without apologies, black sambuca forms an alliance with cocoa, chocolate, and espresso, fulfilling the promise that good things come in small packages.

MAKE THE COCOA SAMBUCA MINI-CAKES   Preheat the oven to 325°F. Line each of 24 miniature muffin cups with mini-size (1⅝ inch) paper or foil bake cups. Set aside.

In a sifter combine the flour, cocoa powder, and baking powder. Sift onto a large piece of parchment paper (or wax paper) and set aside until needed.

Place the sugar, egg, and egg yolk in the bowl of an electric mixer fitted with a paddle. Beat on medium-high speed for 2 minutes until the mixture is slightly thickened and light in color. Operate the mixer on low while slowly adding the butter in a steady stream. Mix until incorporated, about 1 minute. Continue to operate the mixer on low and slowly add the dry ingredients. Mix until incorporated, about 1 minute. Use a rubber spatula to scrape down the sides of the bowl and the paddle. Operate the mixer on low while adding the black sambuca in a slow, steady stream; mix until incorporated, about 30 seconds. Now beat on medium for 30 seconds. Remove the bowl from the mixer and use a rubber spatula to finish mixing the batter until thoroughly combined. (This batter has a fabulous dark chocolate look and, thanks to the sambuca, is unusually fragrant as well. But please do not indulge, as the potential for salmonella is only a finger lick away.)

Portion 1 slightly heaping tablespoon or 1 slightly heaping #70 ice cream scoop of the cake batter into each bake cup. Place the muffin tins on the top and center racks of the oven, and bake until a toothpick inserted in the center of one of the mini-cakes comes out clean, 13 to 14 minutes. (Rotate the tins from top to center halfway through the baking time and turn each 180 degrees.) Remove the mini-cakes from the oven and cool at room temperature in the tins for 10 minutes. Remove the

COCOA SAMBUCA MINI-CAKES

½ cup all-purpose flour
½ cup unsweetened cocoa powder
1 teaspoon baking powder
½ cup granulated sugar
1 large egg
1 large egg yolk
¼ pound (1 stick) unsalted butter, melted
¼ cup black sambuca

MOCHA SAMBUCA GANACHE

4 ounces semisweet baking chocolate, coarsely chopped
⅓ cup heavy cream
3 tablespoons whole espresso beans
½ ounce unsalted butter
1 tablespoon black sambuca
2 teaspoons granulated sugar

GARNISH

24 chocolate-covered espresso beans

MAKES 24 SHOOTERS

mini-cakes from the muffin tins (but not from the paper or foil bake cups), and set aside at room temperature.

PREPARE THE MOCHA SAMBUCA GANACHE   Place the semi-sweet chocolate in a medium bowl. Heat the heavy cream, espresso beans, butter, black sambuca, and sugar in a small saucepan over medium heat. When hot, stir to dissolve the sugar and butter. Bring to a boil. Pour the boiling cream mixture through a strainer held over the chopped chocolate; stir with a whisk until smooth. Transfer the ganache to a baking sheet with sides and spread evenly. Refrigerate the ganache for 45 to 60 minutes until firm to the touch (now you can lick your finger).

Remove the firm ganache from the refrigerator and transfer it to the bowl of an electric mixer fitted with a paddle. Beat on medium speed for 30 seconds until slightly lighter in color. Remove the bowl from the mixer and use a rubber spatula to finish mixing the ingredients until thoroughly combined. Transfer the ganache to a pastry bag fitted with a medium straight tip. Pipe approximately 1 heaping teaspoon of ganache onto each cake. Place a whole chocolate-covered espresso bean onto the ganache on each mini-cake and serve immediately.

☊HE CHEF'S TOUCH

We selected the suave Romana Black Liquore di Sambuca for this recipe. Made in Rome by the same family for more than 125 years, it has a flavor and aroma that will awaken your senses in spite of its turbid appearance.

The Shooters may be prepared over 2 days.

DAY 1: Bake the individual Cocoa Sambuca Mini-Cakes. Once they're cooled, cover with plastic wrap and refrigerate.

DAY 2: Remove the mini-cakes from the refrigerator. Make the Mocha Sambuca ganache. Pipe the ganache onto the mini-cakes as directed in the recipe. Garnish with chocolate-covered espresso beans and serve.

After assembly, you may keep the Shooters in a large, tightly sealed plastic container at room temperature for 2 to 3 days.

DOUBLE CHOCOLATE PECAN TART

When The Trellis pastry chef, Don Mack, crafted the first Death by Chocolate Cake in February 1982, little did he realize how that confection would become the tail that wags the dog. Many other extraordinary chocolate desserts have made the scene at The Trellis over the years, only to be submerged and sometimes forgotten because of the monstrous popularity of Death by Chocolate. This Double Chocolate Pecan Tart was first served on Thanksgiving Day in 1980, the only Thanksgiving we've ever been open. (Just a few days earlier the restaurant had opened to serve its first meal, and we thought it would send the wrong signal to close for a day so soon after opening.) This remains one of my all-time favorite desserts.

MAKE THE TART SHELL   Place 1¼ cups of the flour, the sugar, and the salt in the bowl of an electric mixer fitted with a paddle. Mix on low speed for 15 seconds to combine the ingredients. Add the butter and mix on low for 1½ minutes until the butter is cut into the flour and the mixture develops a mealy texture. Gradually add the milk while mixing on low until the dough comes together, about 30 seconds. Remove the dough (including any that has adhered to the sides of the bowl) from the mixer and form it into a smooth round ball. Wrap in plastic wrap, then press into a 1-inch-thick disk (this makes the subsequent rolling of the dough a bit easier). Place the dough in the freezer for 15 minutes.

Preheat the oven to 375°F.

Remove the dough from the freezer and remove and discard the plastic wrap. Place the dough on a clean, dry, lightly floured work surface. Roll the dough, with a rolling pin that has been dusted with flour (using the remaining ¼ cup of flour as necessary to prevent the dough from sticking), into a circle 13 to 14 inches in diameter and ⅛ inch thick. Line a 9 × 1-inch fluted false bottom tart pan with the dough, gently

TART SHELL DOUGH

1½ cups all-purpose flour

1 tablespoon granulated sugar

½ teaspoon salt

6 tablespoons chilled unsalted butter, cut into 1-tablespoon-size pieces

⅓ cup cold whole milk plus 2 tablespoons

1 cup uncooked rice

DOUBLE CHOCOLATE PECAN FILLING

2½ cups pecan halves

6 ounces semisweet baking chocolate, coarsely chopped

¼ pound (1 stick) unsalted butter, cut into ½-ounce pieces

2 ounces unsweetened baking chocolate, coarsely chopped

8 large egg yolks

¼ cup granulated sugar

SERVES 8

pressing the dough around the bottom and sides of the pan. Use a paring knife or scissors to trim the dough, leaving a ¾-inch border.

Fold the border over and into the sides of the dough in the pan and press gently into place. The folded border should stand about ¼ inch over the top edge of the pan. Prick the dough in the bottom of the pan with the tines of a fork in several evenly spaced places. Refrigerate for 30 minutes.

Line the dough with a 12-inch square of aluminum foil; weigh down the foil with the rice (evenly spread the rice over the surface of the foil). Place on a baking sheet in the center of the oven and bake until the edges of the dough are a light golden brown, about 30 minutes (rotate the pan 180 degrees after 20 minutes). Remove the baked tart shell from the oven; immediately discard the foil and rice. Cool at room temperature while preparing the Double Chocolate Pecan Filling.

PREPARE THE DOUBLE CHOCOLATE PECAN FILLING Preheat the oven to 300°F. Set aside 36 (about ½ cup) of the best-looking pecan halves (these will be placed on top of the filling). Toast the remaining pecan halves on a baking sheet in the oven for 12 minutes. Cool the nuts to room temperature before chopping in a food processor fitted with a metal blade until medium fine, about 10 seconds (you may also chop the pecans by hand, using a cook's knife).

Melt the semisweet chocolate, butter, and unsweetened chocolate in the top half of a double boiler, or in a small glass bowl in a microwave oven (see pages 20–21) and stir until smooth. Set aside until needed.

Place the egg yolks and sugar in the bowl of an electric mixer fitted with a paddle. Beat on medium-high speed for 4 minutes until combined and slightly thickened. Scrape down the sides of the bowl. Add the melted chocolate and butter mixture and mix on medium for 20 seconds. Add the chopped pecans and mix on low for 10 seconds. Remove the bowl from the mixer and use a rubber spatula to finish mixing the scrumptious-looking filling until thoroughly combined.

Transfer the filling to the cooled tart shell, using a rubber spatula to spread it evenly. Arrange a ring of 18 of the reserved pecan halves, rough side up, evenly spaced, on top of the filling, near the inside edge of the tart crust. Arrange a second ring of 12 pecans inside the first ring and then a third ring of 6 pecans in the center. Bake the tart on the center shelf of the oven until the filling is firm to the touch, about 30 minutes. Remove the tart from the oven and allow to cool for 30 to 60 minutes at room temperature before removing it from the pan and serving.

TO SERVE Heat the blade of a serrated slicer under hot running water and wipe the blade dry before making each slice. I love serving white chocolate ice cream (page 127) with this tart, but I won't be insulted if you serve it with your favorite ice cream.

𝒯HE CHEF'S TOUCH

We used a 9 × 1-inch fluted false bottom tart pan for this tart. You may use a slightly smaller or larger pan without altering the recipe. Obviously, the beauty of a pan with a removable bottom is the ease of separating the baked crust from the pan.

Curious? The best-looking pecan halves that you saved to place on top of the filling are not toasted, because they will be exposed to enough heat when the tart is baked to get them exactly as golden brown as desired.

This tart may be prepared over 2 days.

DAY 1: Bake the tart shell as directed. Once it's baked, cool to room temperature, then place in a tightly sealed plastic container at room temperature until the next day.

DAY 2: Make the chocolate filling, then transfer it to the pre-baked tart shell. Top with the reserved pecan halves and bake as directed in the recipe. Cool for 1 hour at room temperature before cutting and serving.

After the tart has cooled, it may be served immediately, or refrigerated for 2 to 3 days in a tightly sealed plastic container (to prevent refrigerator aromas from permeating the tart). Remove the tart from the refrigerator 30 to 60 minutes before serving.

Dr. Chocolate recommends serving the tart slightly warm—place a slice on a plate in the microwave for 45 seconds at medium power, then prepare yourself for a very special chocolate eating experience.

KELLY'S ISLAND CHOCOLATE COCONUT RUM PIE

FLAKY PIE CRUST DOUGH

1/3 cup whole milk

2 large egg yolks

1 tablespoon pure vanilla
  extract

2 cups all-purpose flour

1/4 pound (1 stick) unsalted
  butter, cut into 1/2-ounce
  pieces

CHOCOLATE COCONUT RUM FILLING

1 1/2 cups dried unsweetened
  coconut flakes

1 1/2 cups granulated sugar

1/2 cup dark corn syrup

3 ounces unsalted butter, cut
  into 1/2-ounce pieces

1/4 cup Myers's dark rum

1 teaspoon salt

8 ounces semisweet baking
  chocolate, coarsely
  chopped

5 large eggs

SERVES 8

My wife, Connie, was surprised to see this dessert featured at The Trellis. Connie knows that we favor more dramatic presentations for our chocolate confections. Our Death by Chocolate Cake stands 6 inches tall (and believe me when I tell you that each slice weighs slightly over a pound). Pies as such rarely make an appearance at The Trellis. I know all about mom and apple pie, but it's killer chocolate desserts that put the bacon on the table at my house. So how the heck is it that pastry chef Kelly Bailey came to the conclusion that her Chocolate Coconut Rum Pie merited an appearance at The Trellis? I'll give you a hint, and that is what Connie said when she took her first bite of the pie: "Call 911!"

MAKE THE FLAKY PIE CRUST DOUGH   Place the milk, egg yolks, and vanilla extract in a small bowl. Use a fork to stir the egg and milk mixture until thoroughly combined. Set aside.

Place 1 3/4 cups of the flour and the butter in the bowl of an electric mixer fitted with a paddle. Mix on the lowest speed (stir) for 1 1/2 minutes, until the butter is cut into the flour and the mixture develops a very coarse texture (some small chunks of butter should be visible; if not, you probably have overmixed). Gradually add the milk and egg mixture while mixing on low until the dough comes together, 15 to 20 seconds. Remove the dough from the mixer and form it into a smooth round ball. Wrap in plastic wrap, then press into a 1-inch-thick disk (this makes rolling the dough real easy, especially with a soft dough like this one). Refrigerate the dough for 20 minutes.

Remove the dough from the refrigerator and remove and discard the plastic wrap. Place the dough on a clean, dry, lightly floured work surface. Roll the dough with a rolling pin that has been dusted with flour (use the remaining ¼ cup of flour as necessary to prevent the dough from sticking) into a circle about 16 inches in diameter and ¼ inch thick. Line a 9 × 1½-inch nonstick pie pan with the dough, gently pressing the dough around the bottom and sides of the pan. Use a paring knife or scissors to trim the dough, leaving a 2 inch border. Fold a 3- to 4-inch section of the border at a time, over and into the sides of the dough in the pan, and press gently into place. The folded border should stand about 1 inch from the top edge of the pan. Continue to fold and press the remaining dough border into the pan, a 3- to 4-inch section at a time, until all of the border has been folded into the pan (this creates an impressive-looking wavelike edge). Set aside at room temperature while preparing the filling.

PREPARE THE CHOCOLATE COCONUT RUM FILLING Preheat the oven to 325°F. Toast the coconut flakes on a baking sheet in the oven until golden brown (they will also be crispy after a few seconds out of the oven), about 5 minutes.

Heat the sugar, corn syrup, butter, rum, and salt in a medium saucepan over medium heat. Bring to a boil, stirring frequently while the mixture is heating. Reduce the heat to low and cook the mixture for 1 minute. Remove from the heat; immediately add the semisweet chocolate, stirring constantly until the chocolate is melted and the mixture is smooth (be careful while stirring not to splash the scorching-hot mixture out of the bowl). Set aside until needed in a minute or so.

Place the eggs in the bowl of an electric mixer fitted with a balloon whip. Whisk on medium speed for 1 minute until combined. Operate the mixer on medium while gradually adding the hot chocolate mixture. Mix on medium speed for 1 minute until incorporated. Remove the bowl from the mixer and use a rubber spatula to fold in the coconut flakes until evenly distributed.

Pour the chocolate and coconut mixture into the prepared pie shell. Place the pie pan on a baking sheet on the center rack in the oven and bake for 1 hour, until the crust is golden brown and the chocolate center is domed and shiny. Remove the pie from the oven and cool at room temperature for 30 minutes. Refrigerate the pie for 8 hours before cutting and serving.

TO SERVE   Heat the blade of a serrated knife with a rounded tip under hot running water and wipe the blade dry before cutting each slice. Consider serving the pie with rum-flavored unsweetened whipped cream.

*T*HE CHEF'S TOUCH

You will find dried unsweetened coconut flakes in the bulk food section at the supermarket, usually near the dried fruits or nuts. Stay away from other types of packaged coconut for this recipe.

I specify Myers's rum from Jamaica because it imparts a bold but smooth buttery flavor in desserts; it's also outstanding as a beverage. This remarkable rum is aged in white oak barrels, and it is during this aging that Myers's acquires its distinctly dark color.

After assembly, you may keep Kelly's Island Chocolate Coconut Rum Pie in the refrigerator for 2 days before serving. To avoid permeating the pie with refrigerator odors, place it in a large, tightly sealed plastic container.

Woozy Chocolate Brioche French Toast with Oozy Chocolate Maple Syrup

When I was a kid, you couldn't get me near a piece of French toast. I just was not enamored with the appearance, the aroma, and especially the texture of these egg-soaked pieces of white bread. For me it was a jar of peanut butter and an electric toaster that transformed white bread into something desirable. Later, as a marine, it was one of the things that I passed up in the mess hall—even hunger pangs couldn't convert me. It was left to the diabolically clever culinary mind of Ganache Hill test kitchen chef Brett Bailey to fashion a French toast that would have me chewing passionately what I previously eschewed.

MAKE THE COCOA CHOCOLATE CHIP BRIOCHE   Lightly coat the inside of a 9 × 5 × 3-inch loaf pan with the melted butter. Set aside.

In a sifter combine the flour, cocoa powder, and salt. Sift onto a large piece of parchment paper (or wax paper) and set aside until needed.

Place the ¼ pound butter in a small glass bowl in a microwave oven set at medium power for 55 seconds. Remove from the microwave oven, and use a rubber spatula to stir the butter until melted, smooth, and creamy (this will take several minutes of stirring but will yield a butter with a sauce-like consistency as well as a melted butter that is not warm—it must not be warm when it is added to the dough). Set aside.

In a small bowl whisk together the eggs and vanilla extract. Set aside.

In the bowl of an electric mixer, dissolve 1 tablespoon of the sugar in ¼ cup warm water (100° to 110°F). Add the yeast and stir gently to dissolve. Allow the mixture to stand and foam for 4 to 5 minutes (the foam should get slightly puffy).

Add the egg and vanilla mixture to the foaming sugar and yeast, followed by the dry ingredients and the ¼ cup sugar. Combine on the low

COCOA CHOCOLATE CHIP BRIOCHE

1 teaspoon unsalted butter, melted

¼ pound (1 stick) unsalted butter, cut into ½-ounce pieces

2½ cups all-purpose flour

½ cup unsweetened cocoa powder

1 teaspoon salt

3 large eggs

1 tablespoon pure vanilla extract

¼ cup granulated sugar plus 1 tablespoon

¼ cup warm water

3 tablespoons dry active yeast

½ cup chocolate mini-morsels

OOZY CHOCOLATE MAPLE SYRUP

6 ounces semisweet baking chocolate, melted (see pages 20–21)

¾ cup 100% pure U.S.
   Grade A dark amber
   maple syrup

WOOZY WHISKEY EGG DIP
3 large eggs
¼ cup bourbon whiskey
3 tablespoons half-and-half
2 tablespoons granulated
   sugar

MAKES 12 SLICES

speed of an electric mixer fitted with a dough hook for 1 minute. Use a rubber spatula to scrape down the sides of the bowl, then continue to mix on low speed until the ingredients have combined to form a spongy dough, about 2 minutes. Add about half of the creamy melted butter to the dough and mix on medium-low speed for 1½ minutes until the butter has been thoroughly absorbed by the dough. Add the remaining butter and continue to mix on medium-low speed until the butter has been absorbed and the dough forms a solid mass and cleans the inside of the bowl, about 3 minutes. Add the chocolate mini-morsels and mix on low speed to incorporate, about 45 seconds.

Remove the dough from the mixer and form it into a log shape measuring 9 inches long and 3 inches wide. Place the log in the prepared loaf pan, cover with a dry towel, place in a warm location, and allow to rise until the dough has doubled in volume, about 1½ hours (the time will vary depending on the warmth of the space. An ambient temperature of 80° to 90°F would be good; depending on the time of the year, consider a screened porch or even the backseat of your automobile).

Once the dough has doubled in volume, use your fingers to gently punch down the dough about ½ inch. Cover the pan with a dry towel and place in a warm location so the dough can rise until it has almost doubled in volume, for the second time, about 1½ hours (again, this may take longer if your kitchen is very cool).

Preheat the oven to 325°F.

Bake the brioche in the oven for 40 minutes until firm and hollow-sounding when gently tapped on the top. Immediately remove the loaf from the pan (it will turn out easily) and cool on a wire rack at room temperature before slicing, about 1 hour.

MAKE THE OOZY CHOCOLATE MAPLE SYRUP Place the semi-sweet chocolate in a small bowl, then add the syrup and stir vigorously with a handheld whisk to combine. Set aside.

MAKE THE WOOZY WHISKEY EGG DIP In a medium bowl whisk together the eggs, bourbon whiskey, half-and-half, and sugar. Set aside.

DIP IN THE WOOZY AND DRIZZLE ON THE OOZY Slice the brioche loaf into 12 slices ¾ inch thick. Heat a large nonstick sauté pan over medium heat. When the pan is hot, quickly dip (don't soak) each side of a piece of brioche in the egg dip, then place the brioche in the hot pan; repeat with additional slices (you should be able to cook 3 to 4 pieces of brioche at a time). Cook the brioche slice for 1 to 1½ minutes on each side until golden brown and hot. Remove the French toast from the pan and hold in a 200°F oven while cooking the remaining slices.

Serve 1 to 2 slices of French toast per person (depending on the time of day and the intent of the occasion) and drizzle an extravagant amount of Oozy Chocolate Maple Syrup over the top of each slice. Serve immediately.

𝒯HE CHEF'S TOUCH

The Oozy Chocolate Maple Syrup may be cooled and then refrigerated in a tightly sealed plastic container for several days. For French toast, you may reheat the syrup. As suggested above, the syrup may also be applied as a chilled spread.

After being baked and cooled to room temperature, the chocolate brioche may be refrigerated for 2 to 3 days or frozen for several weeks. To prevent the brioche from being permeated by refrigerator or freezer odors, place it in a large, tightly sealed plastic container, or wrap well with plastic wrap.

Whether you decide to be traditional and enjoy our French toast for dessert or to start your day with it as a hedonistic breakfast, I suggest a very dry sparkling wine as the appropriate beverage.

HOT CHOCOLATE BUCCANEER

¾ pound semisweet baking
    chocolate, coarsely
    chopped
1 cup spiced rum
½ cup heavy cream
¼ cup granulated sugar
3 cups brewed full-strength
    hot coffee

MAKES **6** DRINKS

Chocolate, rum, cream, sugar, and coffee seem to be a natural composition of flavors. The Buccaneer is a beverage that will lighten the spirit after a difficult day, or warm the soul on the coldest night.

Place the semisweet chocolate, rum, heavy cream, and sugar in a large saucepan. Use a rubber spatula to stir the ingredients until combined. Pour the coffee into the saucepan and stir with a handheld whisk until smooth and well combined. Heat the mixture over medium heat for 6 minutes until hot but not hotter than 150°F (if the mixture gets too hot, the alcohol will evaporate, diminishing the swashbuckling effect of the drink). Serve immediately in warm mugs.

THE CHEF'S TOUCH

Select Captain Morgan Original Spiced Rum from Puerto Rico and you will be rewarded with a smooth liquid infused with a spiciness that will captivate and indulge your palate.

The Hot Chocolate Buccaneer mixture may be cooled to room temperature, then refrigerated for 2 to 3 days before reheating. You may reheat all of the mixture at once, or individually in a mug in the microwave oven. Whatever reheating method you choose, remember— not too hot!

Online Sources

www.dessertstodiefor.com: This is your destination for the most outrageously delicious chocolate cookies imaginable from The Trellis restaurant in Williamsburg, Virginia (this is an unabashed plug for my cookies).

www.ecookbooks.com: This is the website for Jessica's Biscuit, a catalogue house that asserts it has the world's largest cookbook inventory. If you can't find the title here, you had better contact an antiquarian bookseller. Most titles are dramatically discounted.

www.honey.com: Check out this fascinating website for information on specialty honeys and where to purchase them.

www.kingarthurflour.com: We purchased all of the flour used for testing the recipes in this cookbook in supermarkets. But if you need to locate organic flour or any other specialty flour, chances are King Arthur has it in inventory (Trellis pastry chef Kelly Bailey is a big fan). This site also offers specialty pans and tools.

www.KitchenAid.com: If you are looking to upgrade your table model electric mixer, you can do it here with confidence that you are buying the best. Lots of great colors and a variety of power options, from 250 watts to 525 watts—vroom, vroom!

www.surlatable.com: One of my favorite websites. An amazing offering of anything and everything a cook or professional chef would want in the kitchen.

www.Williams-Sonoma.com: A tony website for kitchen fanatics who don't mind paying for the best. Great layout, lots of information, and a wide selection of upscale kitchenware.

www.wilton.com: This should be your first stop for specialty cake pans. The site also has information on available cake decorating classes.

BIBLIOGRAPHY

Amendola, Joseph. *The Bakers' Manual for Quantity Baking and Pastry Making*. New York: Aherns Publishing Company, 1960.

Ayto, John. *The Diner's Dictionary: Food and Drink from A to Z*. Oxford and New York: Oxford University Press, 1993.

Beranbaum, Rose Levy. *The Cake Bible*. New York: William Morrow, 1988.

Bloom, Carol. *The International Dictionary of Desserts, Pastries, and Confections*. New York: Hearst Books, 1995.

Braker, Flo. *The Simple Art of Perfect Baking*. New York: William Morrow, 1985.

Coe, Susan D., and Michael D. Coe. *The True History of Chocolate*. New York: Thames and Hudson, 1996.

Corriher, Shirley O. *Cookwise*. New York: William Morrow, 1998.

Davidson, Alan. *The Oxford Companion to Food*. New York: Oxford University Press, 1999.

Desaulniers, Marcel. *Death by Chocolate*. New York: Rizzoli, 1992.

——. *Desserts to Die For*. New York: Simon & Schuster, 1995.

——. *Death by Chocolate Cakes*. New York: William Morrow, 2000.

Etlinger, Steven, and Irena Chalmers. *The Kitchenware Book*. New York: Macmillan, 1993.

Greenspan, Dorie. *Baking with Julia*. New York: William Morrow, 1996.

Herbst, Sharon Tyler. *The New Food Lover's Companion*. New York: Barron's, 1995.

Knight, John B. *Knight's Foodservice Dictionary*. New York: Van Nostrand Reinhold, 1987.

Lipinski, Robert A., and Kathleen A. Lipinski. *The Complete Beverage Dictionary*. New York: Van Nostrand Reinhold, 1992.

Malgieri, Nick. *How to Bake*. New York: HarperCollins, 1995.

Mariani, John. *The Dictionary of American Food & Drink*. New Haven and New York: Ticknor & Fields, 1983.

Medrich, Alice. *Cocolat*. New York: Warner Books, 1990.

Mimifie, Bernard W. *Chocolate, Cocoa, and Confectionary: Science and Technology*. New York: Van Nostrand Reinhold, 1989.

Ortiz, Elisabeth Lambert. *The Encyclopedia of Herbs, Spices & Flavorings*. New York: Dorling Kindersley, 1992.

Rombauer, Irma S., Marion Rombauer Becker, and Ethan Becker. *The All New All Purpose Joy of Cooking*. New York: Scribner, 1997.

Teubner, Christian. *The Chocolate Bible*. New York: Penguin Studio, 1997.

Walter, Carole. *Great Cakes*. New York: Ballantine Books, 1991.

Wolf, Burt, Emily Aronson, and Florence Fabricant. *The New Cooks' Catalogue*. New York: Alfred A. Knopf, 2000.

Wood, Rebecca. *The New Whole Foods Encyclopedia*. New York: Prentice Hall Press, 1988.

INDEX

I

J

K

L

lemon balm–white chocolate icing, slammin'
citrus squares with, 89–91

M

Madras cake, chocolate, 51–54
Madras cocktail, 54
maple-almond buttercream, 25–27
maple syrup:
  oozy chocolate, 157–58
  oozy chocolate, woozy chocolate brioche
    French toast with, 157–59
marshmallows, coffee-cocoa, 80–81
marshmallow squares, Granny's
    chocolate-and-walnut-covered
    coffee-cocoa, 80–82
masquerade ice cream terrine, caramel
    orange–chocolate orange,
    105–7
microwave ovens, 9
  melting chocolate in, 20–21
mint-julep pop, cocoa, 129–30
mixers, electric, 8
mocha sambuca ganache, 149–50
mocha sambuca shooters, 149–50
mousse:
  bombe, frozen chocolate oh-honey
    so-fluffy, 131–34
  cake, chocolate orange, 51
  chocolate apricot pudding, perfections
    with chocolate-drenched cashews,
    137–40

chocolate pudding, 137–38
chocolate so-fluffy, 131–33
cocoa berry yogurt, 136
pudding, chocolate, 137
white chocolate, 55–57
Mrs. D's "she ain't heavy" chocolate cake,
    36–38
muffin pan, cast-iron, seasoning of,
    72

N

nuts, 22–23
  toasting of, 23
  see also specific nuts

O

offset spatulas, 11
old-world cocoa sponge cake, 42–44
1-2-3 cookie crust, 89–90
oozy chocolate maple syrup, 157–58
oozy chocolate maple syrup, woozy
    chocolate French toast with,
    157–59
orange:
  caramel–, chocolate orange masquerade ice
    cream terrine, 105–7
  caramel ice cream, 105–6
  chocolate masquerade, 105–7
  chocolate mousse cake, 51–52

rummies, chocolate-chunk pineapple, 97–98

rum-raisin-chocolate-banana ice cream cakes with rum and almond twinkle, 108–12

rum-raisin-chocolate cakes, 108–10

S

sambuca ganache, mocha, 149

sambuca shooters, mocha, 149–50

sandwich, chocolate grasshopper ice cream, 117–20

saucepans, 10–11

schnappy chocolate cake, 33–34

"she ain't heavy" chocolate cake, 36–38

shooters, mocha sambuca, 149–50

shortcakes, cocoa cinnamon chocolate chip, 71–72

sifting dry ingredients, 22

slammin' citrus squares with white chocolate–lemon balm icing, 89–91

snow day cakes, 73–74

sparkling cream, 95

sparkling cream, champagne fritters with chocolate grape surprise and, 94–96

spatulas, 11

sponge cake:

cocoa, 48–49

old-world cocoa, 42–44

toasted hazelnut, 30–32

stars and stripes garnish, 127–28

strawberries, frosted, 136

stump cake (chocolate hazelnut Christmas tree stump), 29–32

sugar, brown, *see* brown sugar

sugar cookie base, vanilla, 42–43

super citrus center, 89–90

syrup:

chocolate brandy swirl, 121

oozy chocolate maple, 157–58

oozy chocolate maple, woozy brioche French toast with, 157–59

T

tart, double chocolate pecan, 151–53

tart shell dough, 151–52

techniques, 19–23

thermometers, 12

toasted:

almond bark, chocolate-in-paradise, 145–46

hazelnut sponge cake, 30–32

toasting nuts, 23

toot, toot, toot C-rolls, 141–42

triple chocolate hazelnut bark, 29

truffle cake, chocolate, 131–32

truffles, chocolate, 143

U

utility turners, 11

V

vanilla sugar cookie base, 42–43

W

walnut(s):
    and chocolate coating, 81–82
    -and-chocolate-covered coffee-cocoa
        marshmallow squares, Granny's,
        80–82
    corn flakes crust, 68
    quintessential chocolate ganache with,
        52–53
wax paper, 10
whipped cream, 43, 46
whipped dark chocolate icing,
    29–30
whiskey egg dip, woozy, 158
whisks, 12
white chocolate:
    bread dough, 77
    -butterscotch cookies, 102–3

ice cream, 127–28
as ingredient, 17
-lemon balm icing, 89–91
-lemon balm icing, slammin' citrus squares
    with, 89–91
melted, as garnish, 66–67
mousse, 55–57
pumpkin cheesecakes, 68–69
pumpkin cheesecakes with blackberry
    pixilation, 68–70
White Russian cocktail, 144
White Russian ganache, 143
White Russians, 143–44
woozy chocolate brioche French toast
    with oozy chocolate maple syrup,
    157–59
woozy whiskey egg dip, 158

Y

yogurt mousse:
    cocoa, 136
    cocoa berry, 136

ABOUT THE AUTHOR

MARCEL DESAULNIERS, the "Guru of Ganache," is the executive chef and co-owner of the Trellis Restaurant in Williamsburg, Virginia. He graduated from the Culinary Institute of America in 1965. Marcel has received several national awards, including *Food and Wine*'s Honor Roll of American Chefs, the Who's Who of Food and Beverage in America, the prestigious Ivy Award from *Restaurants and Institutions*, the 1993 James Beard Award for Best American Chef Mid-Atlantic States, the highly coveted Silver Palate Award from the International Foodservice Manufacturers Association, and the 1999 James Beard Award for Outstanding Pastry Chef in America. Marcel is the author of many books, including *Death by Chocolate*, *Desserts to Die For*, *An Alphabet of Sweets*, *Death by Chocolate Cookies*, and, most recently, *Death by Chocolate Cakes*. No chef is more qualified or more passionate about chocolate than America's number one expert, Marcel Desaulniers.